Chivalry Lives In You

Coloring With Kindness

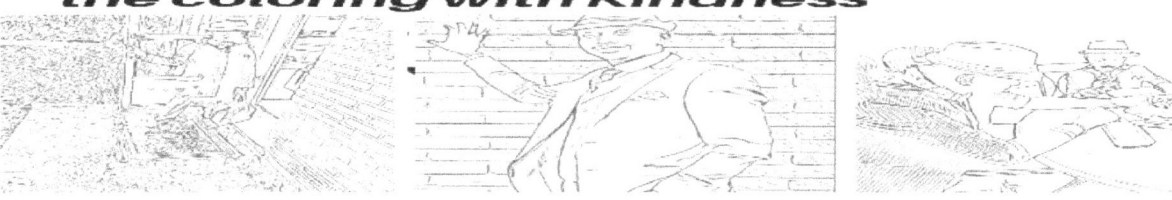

Chivalry Lives In You
Richard Patterson III

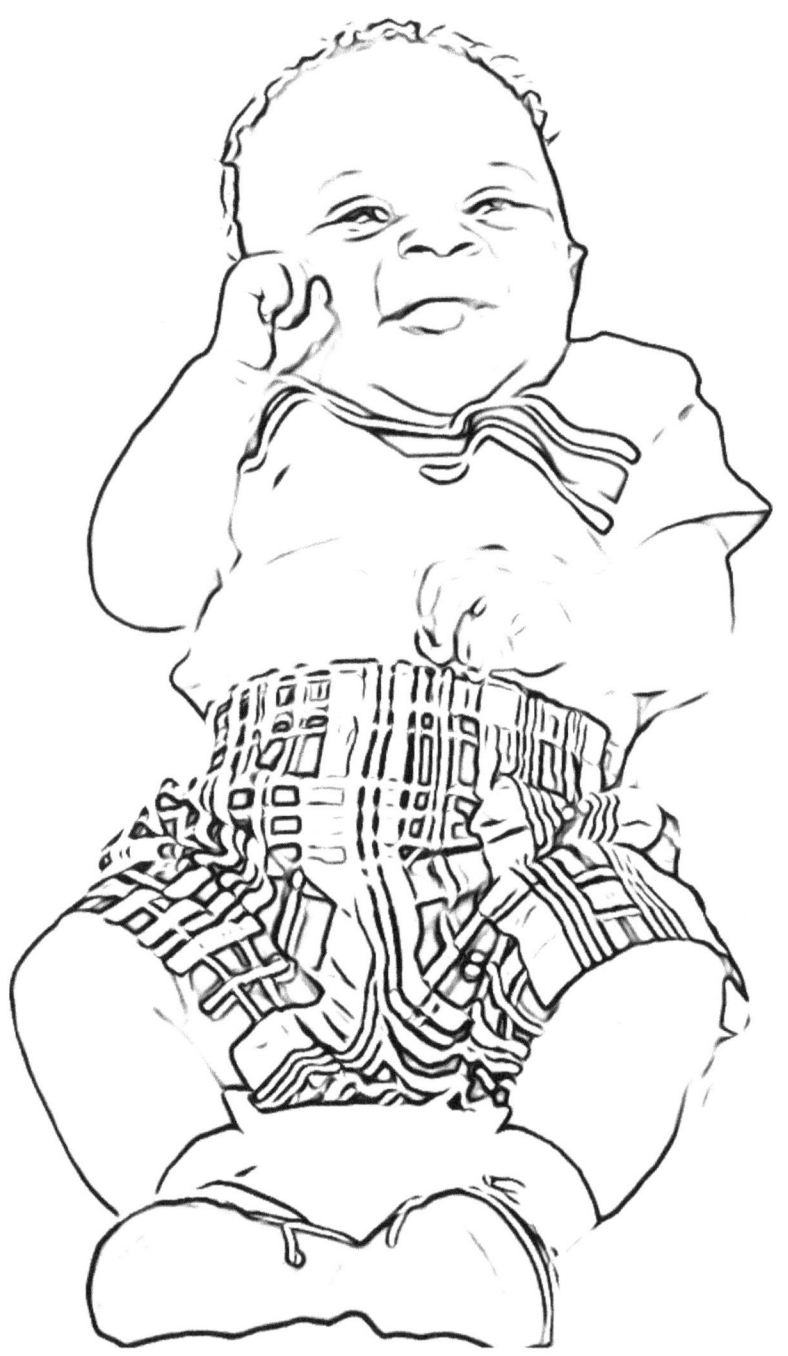

Becoming A Father changed my life. My mother taught me to consider people but when my son was born I had one goal. Teach him your values and don't try and reinvent the wheel. Trust what you were taught

Chivalry Lives In You
Richard Patterson III

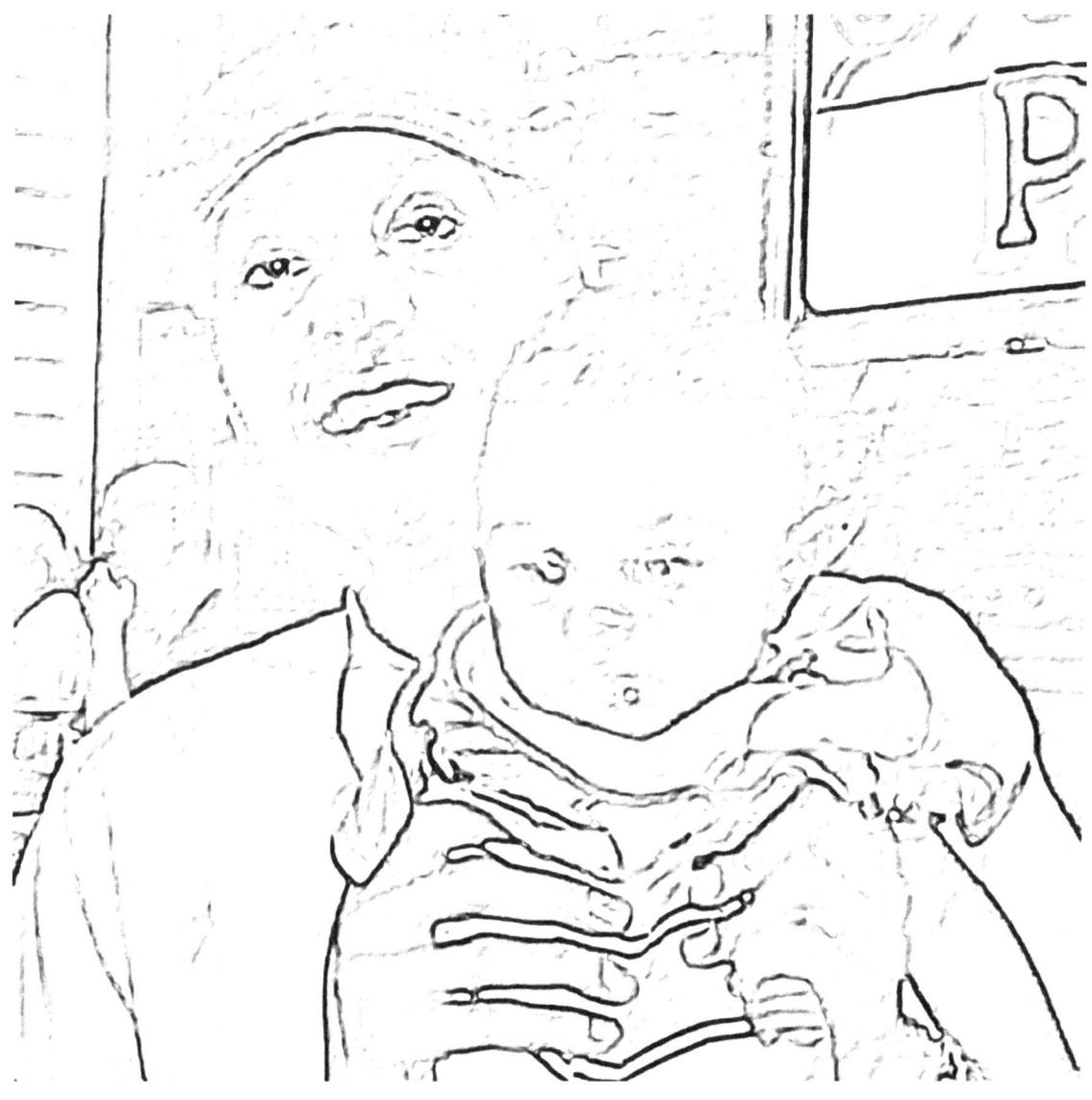

You may think chivalry starts with a door being opened for someone else. While that's an expression, the root is a genuine concern for human life. Like a baby you are careful, handling them with care. The same goes for chivalry "All People have value" that's where you start.

Chivalry Lives In You
Richard Patterson III

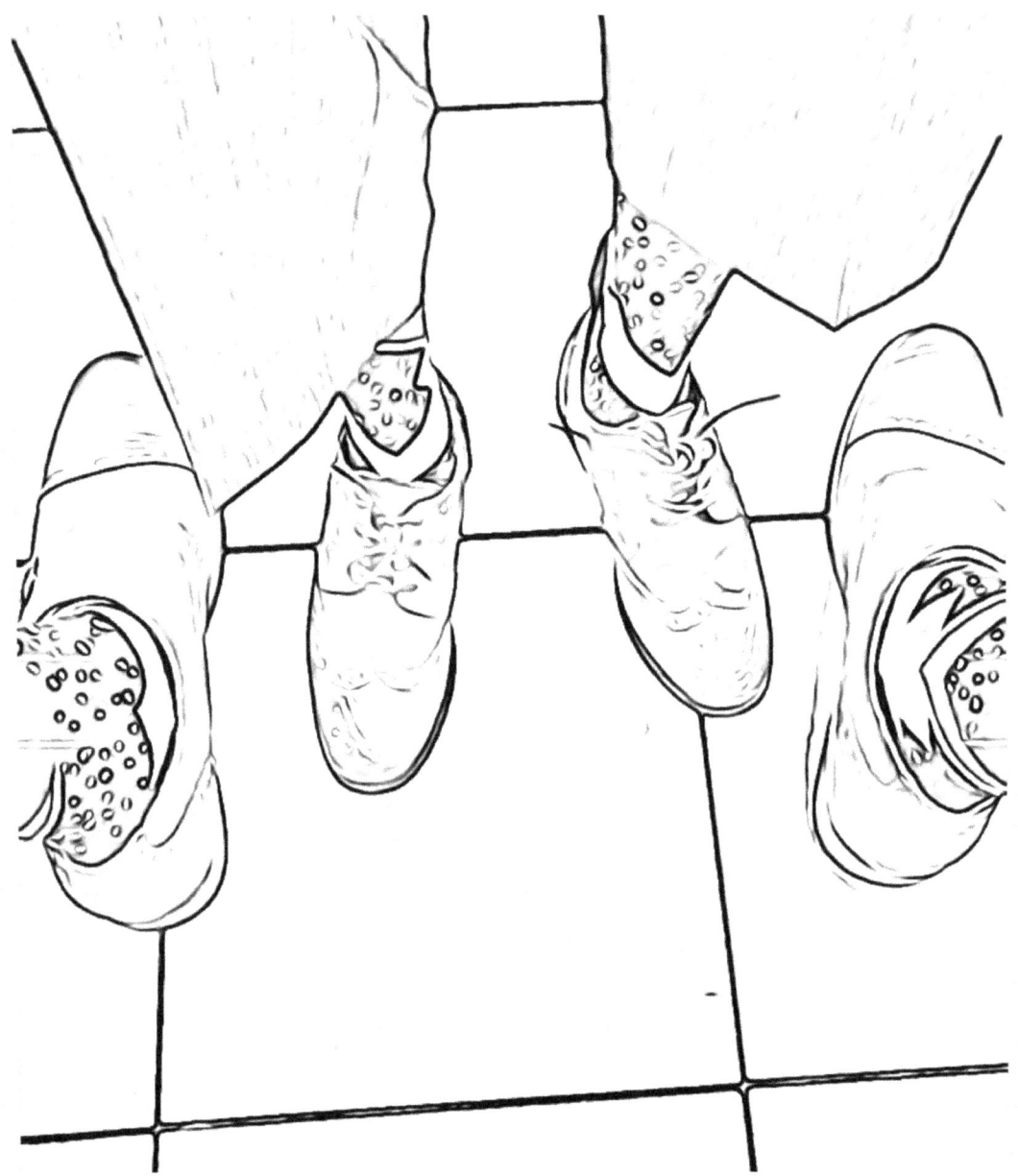

I wanted my son to know that although he has his own path. There are some staples to manhood, one being your ability to admire those who have lived longer than you. Ask questions until you feel good about life, then start walking. Chivalry has admiration for the experiences of others.

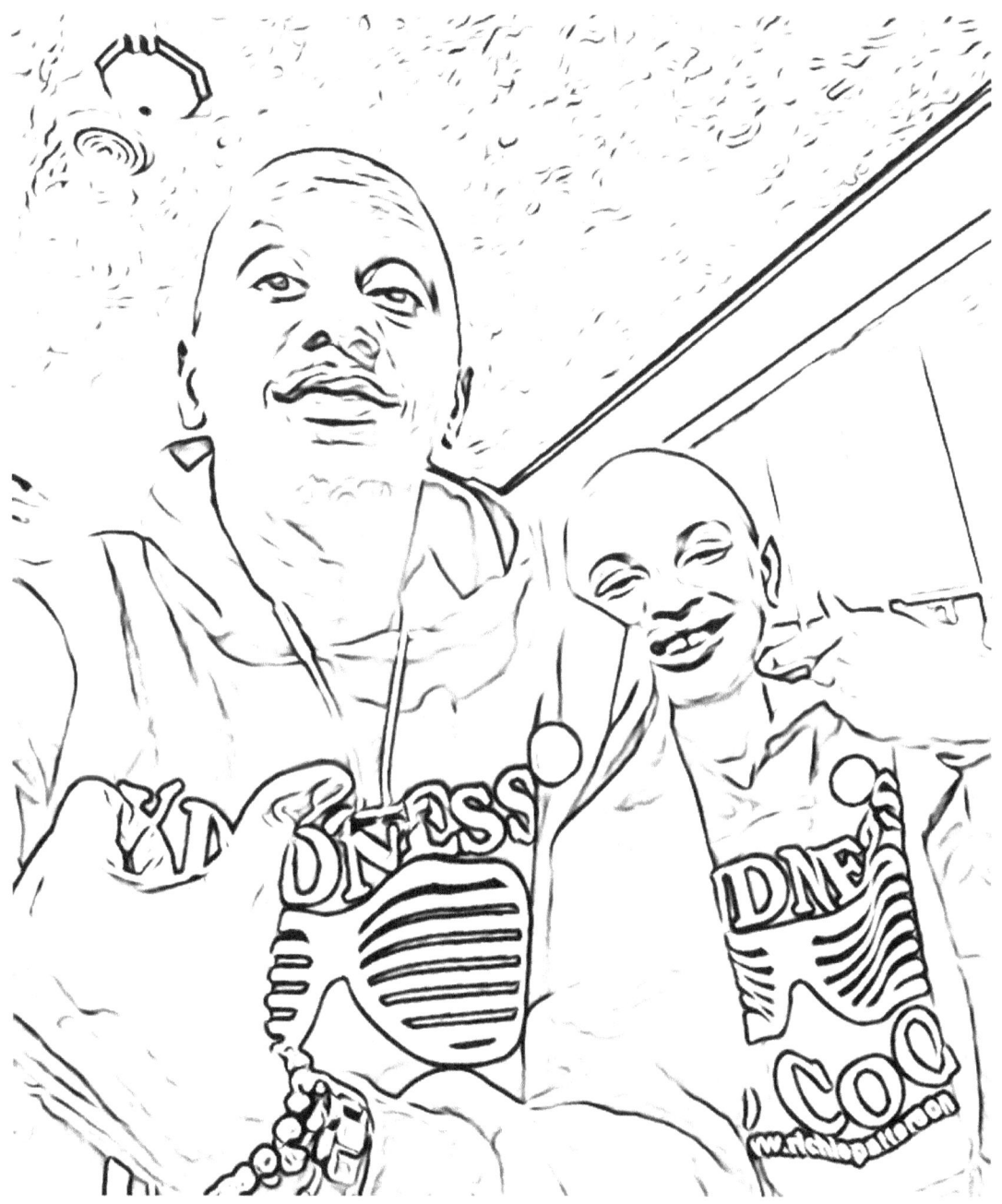

Spending time with my son has a lot to do with sitting down while waiting on services. During this time we people watch and he gets to see what patience looks like. Chivalry is an approach not a reaction.

Chivalry Lives In You
Richard Patterson III

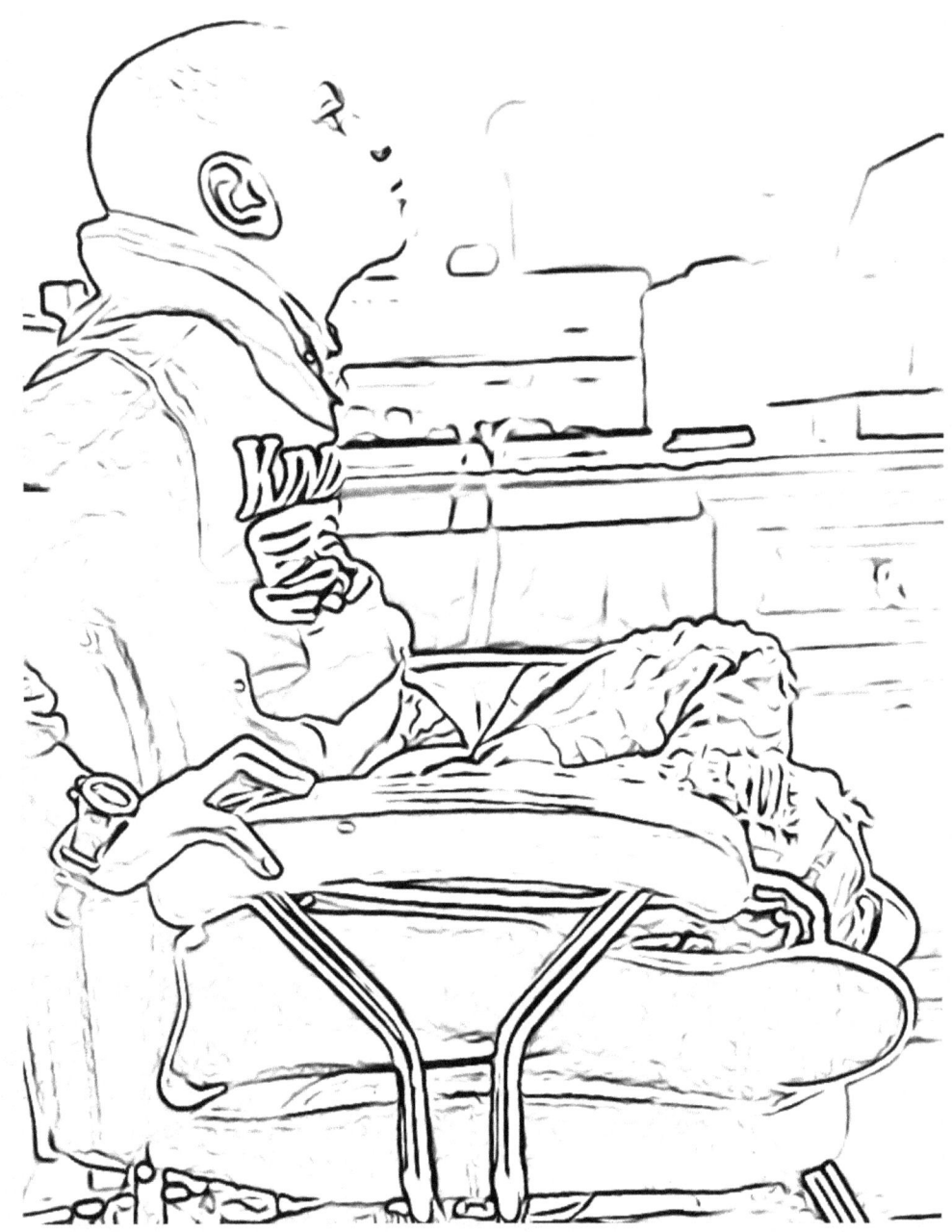

When we are out and about we don't use tablets or technology but we engage with the environment. Reading magazines and talking to people in the environment. Chivalry is never disengaged.

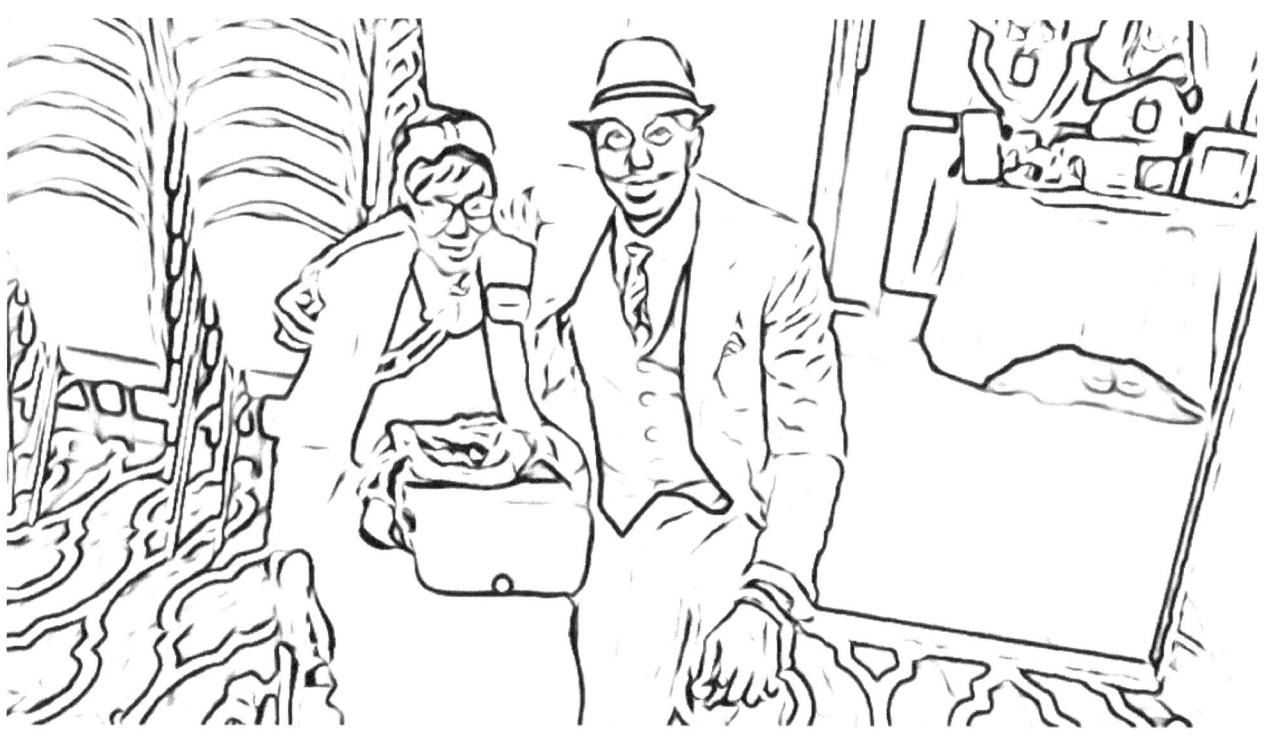

Every elderly person deserves the right to be heard. I choose to slow down on purpose to hear what they have to say. Chivalry pays homage to those who have come before you.

Chivalry Lives In You
Richard Patterson III

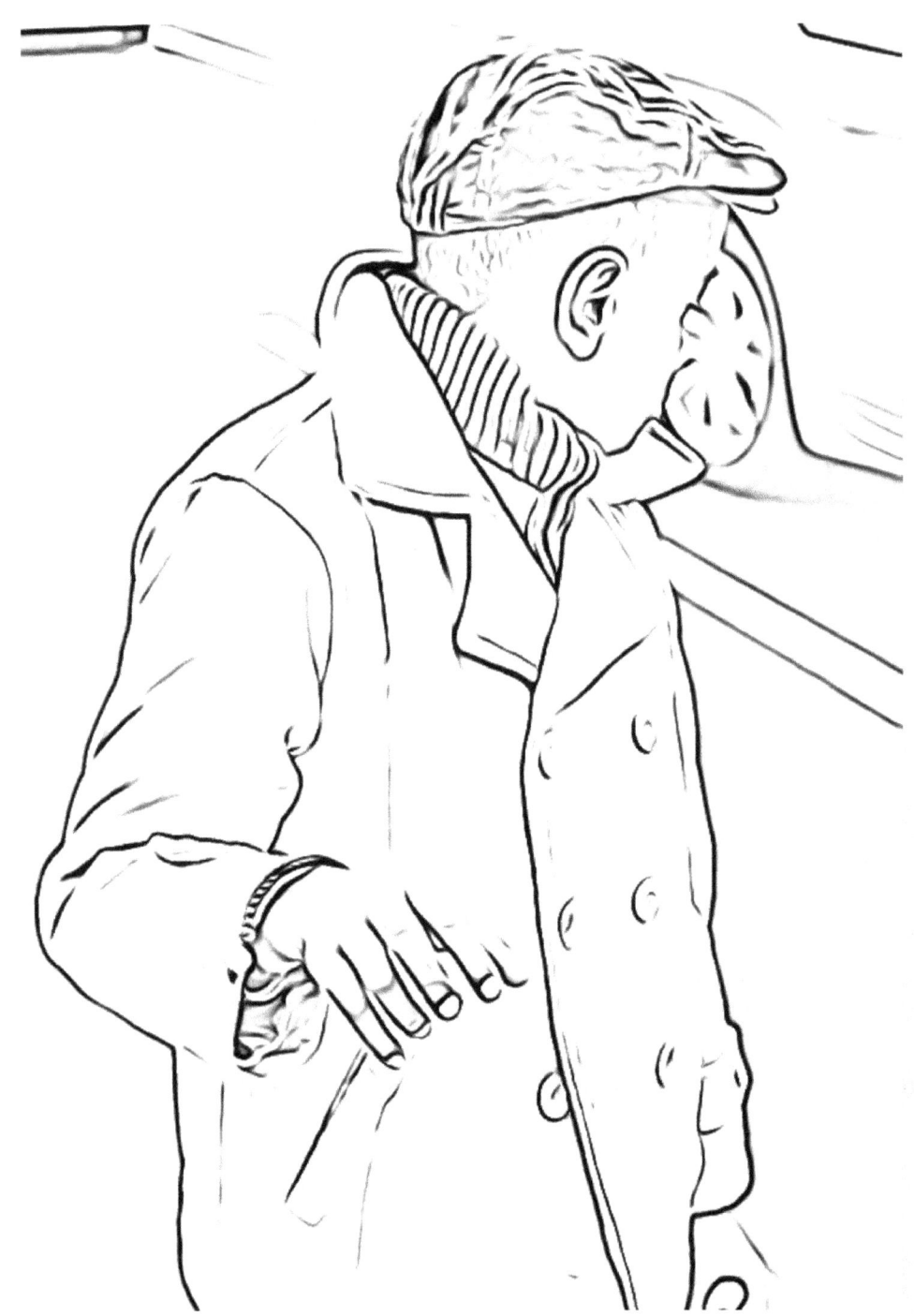

Chivalry takes the initiative to see about those in need. Always look back because someone could require your assistance.

Chivalry Lives In You
Richard Patterson III

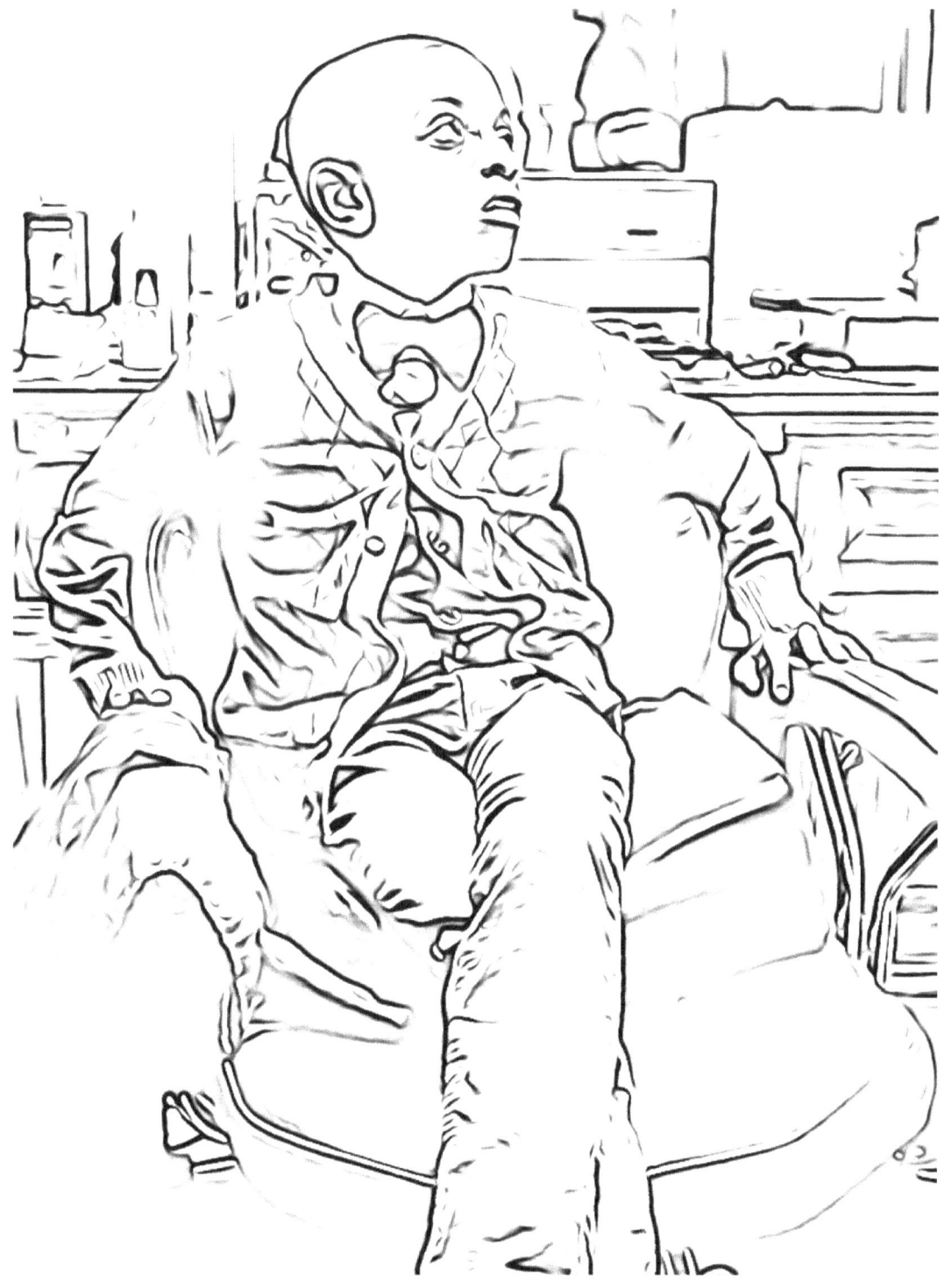

The Barber shop is for hair maintenance. Chivalry is life's maintenance (Considering People)

Chivalry Lives In You
Richard Patterson III

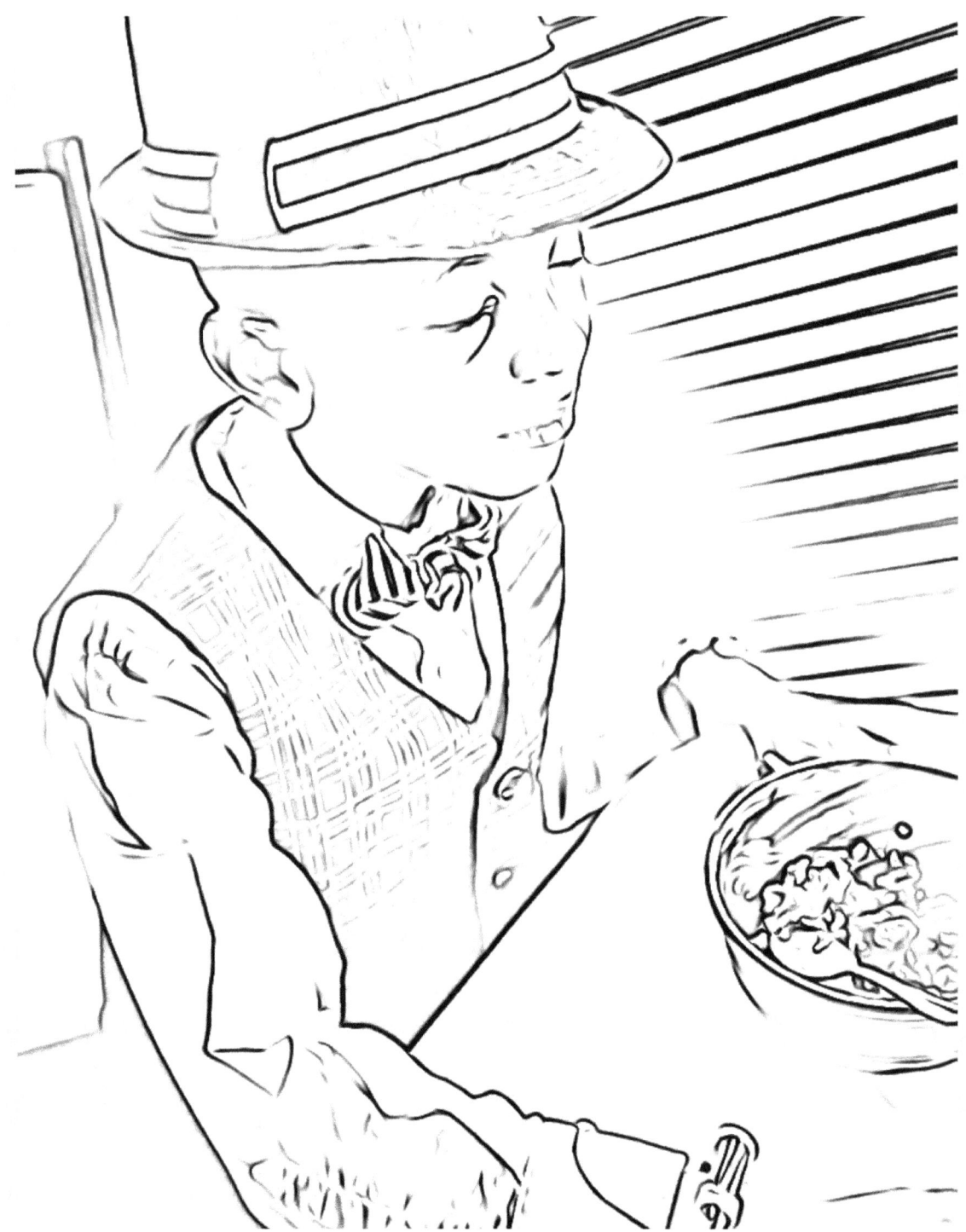

We pray over our food consistently. Chivalry is seeing outside of yourself to make things better like Prayer.

Coloring With Kindness , Page 10

Chivalry Lives In You
Richard Patterson III

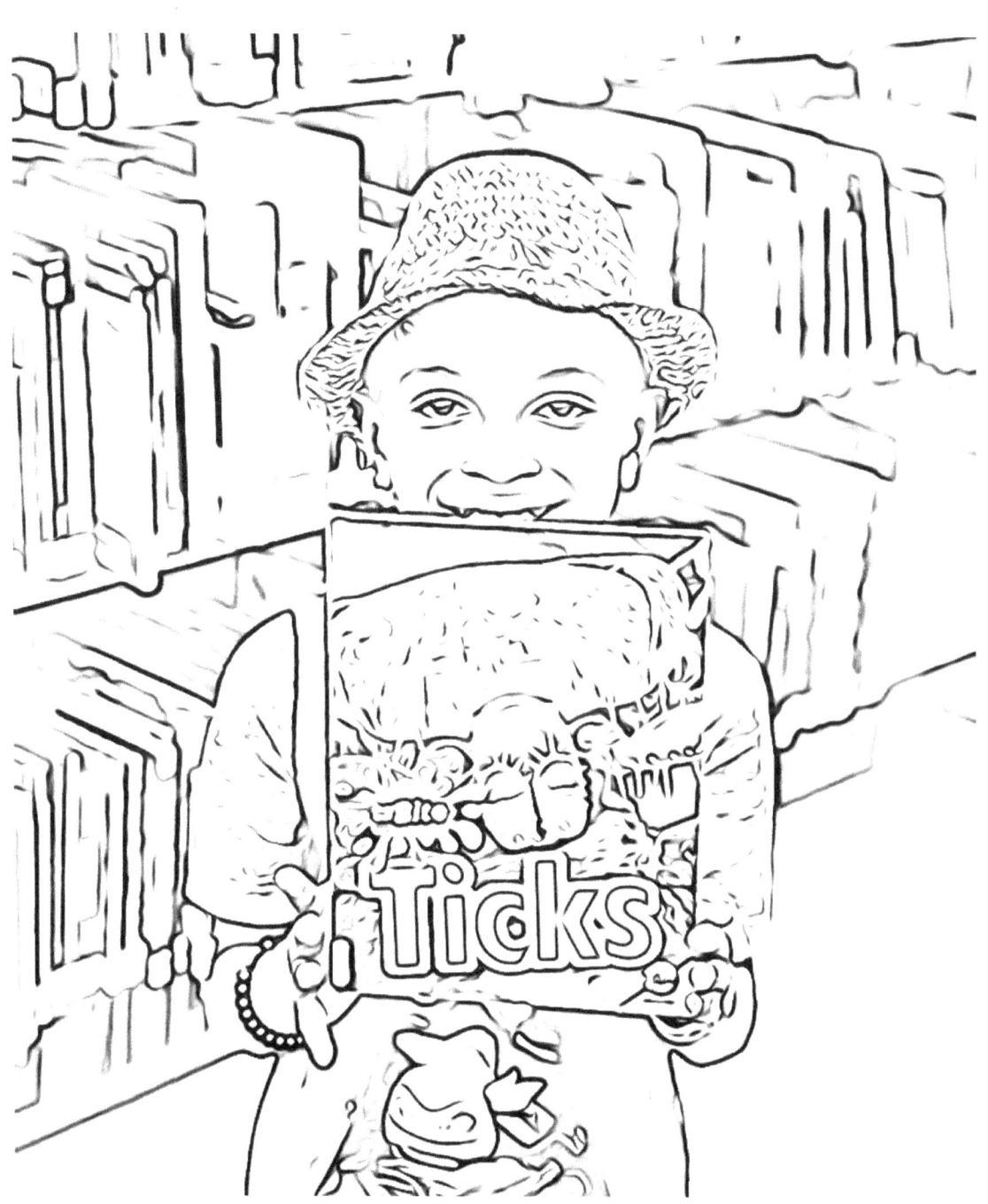

Trips to the library are essential as my son loves animals and insects. Chivalry like the library requires a willingness to understand people as an approach.

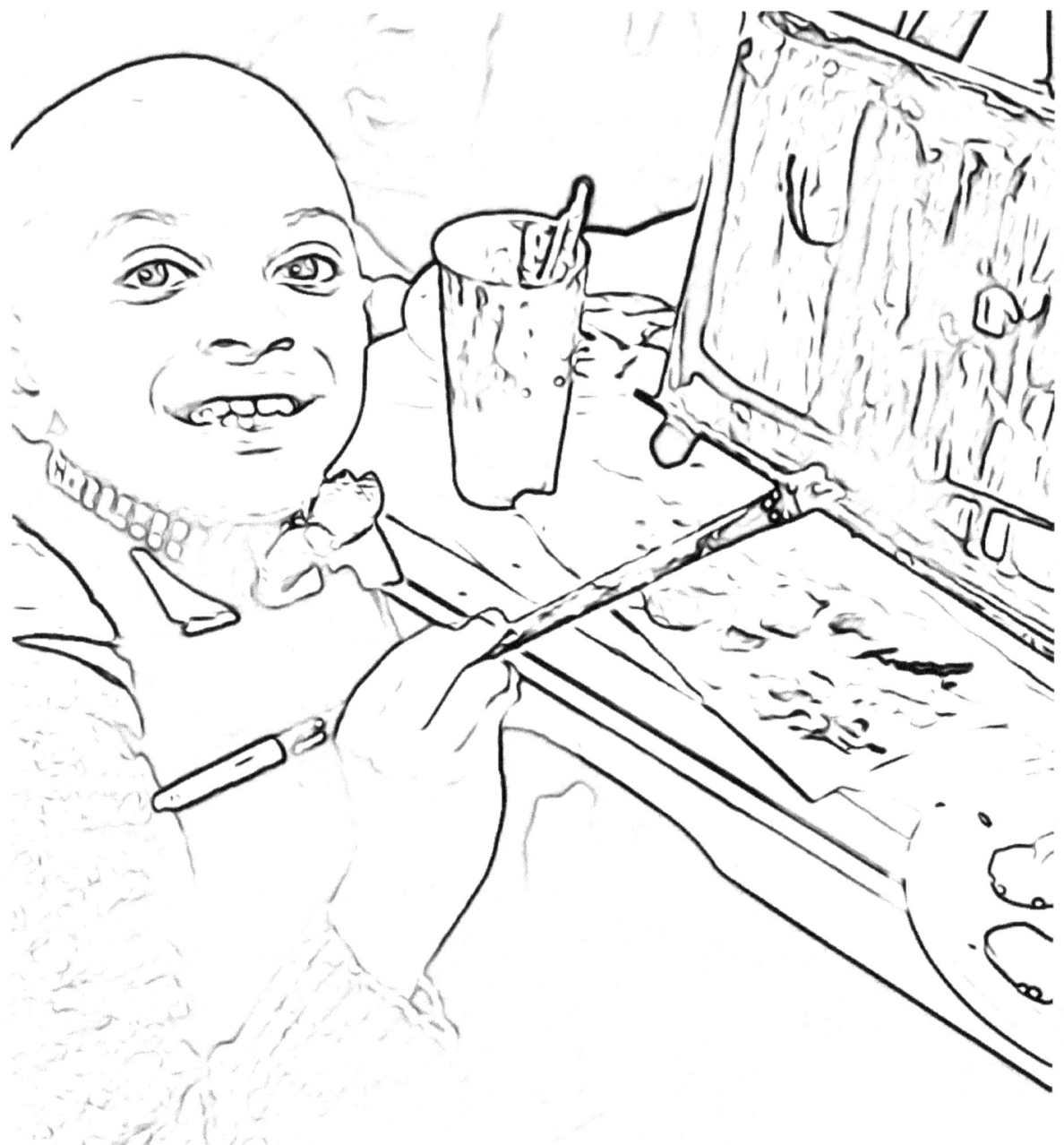

We should always cultivate the creativity in our children and celebrate it. I thank my son when he holds the door open for myself or anyone. Chivalry grows when its acknowledged appropriately.

Chivalry Lives In You
Richard Patterson III

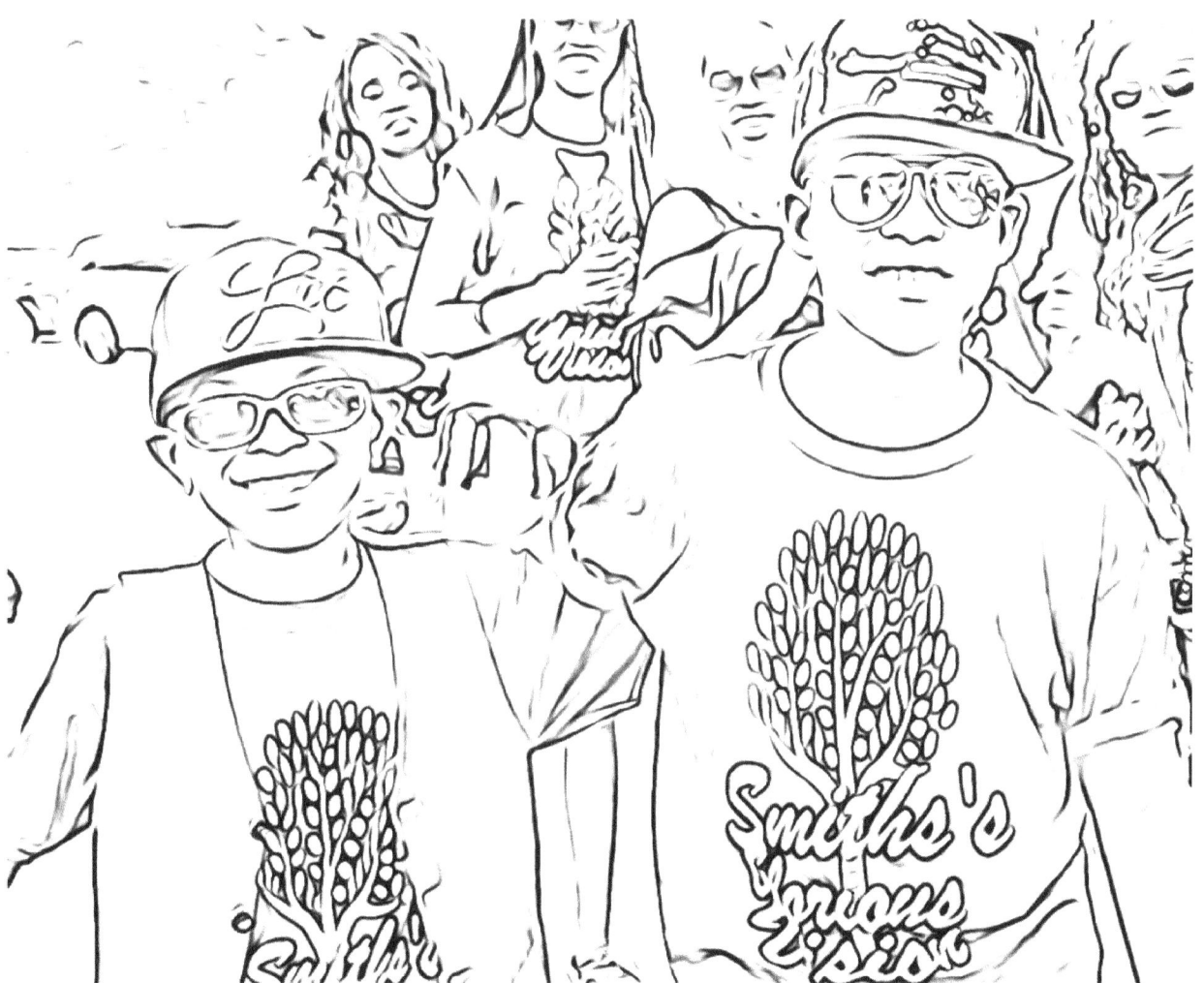

Mutual respect for peers, friends and family. Chivalry is always mindful that attitude is everything.

Chivalry Lives In You
Richard Patterson III

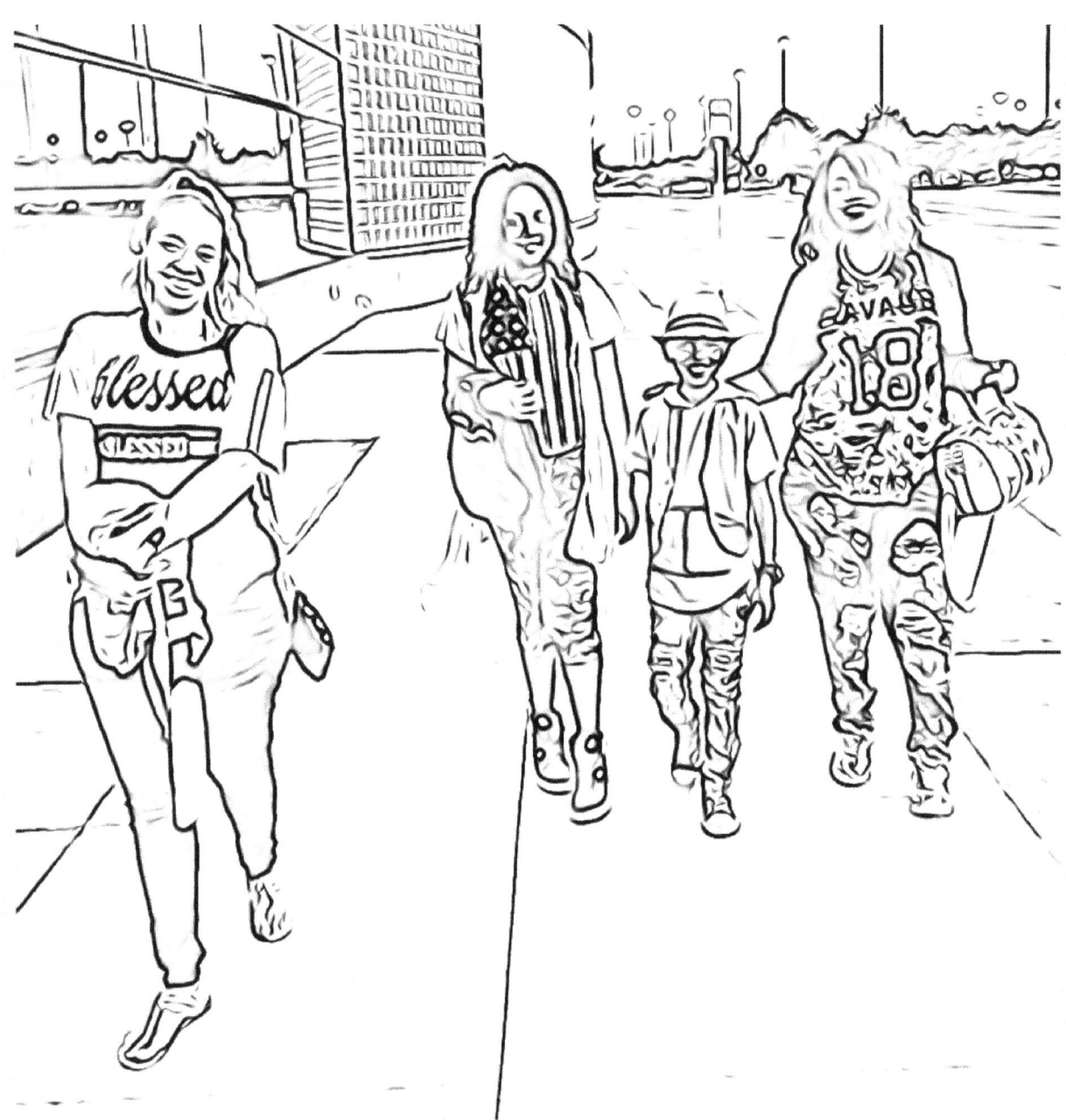

It's important to put children in position to express their care for people. Chivalry is cultivated through good family relationships.

Coloring With Kindness , Page 14

Chivalry Lives In You
Richard Patterson III

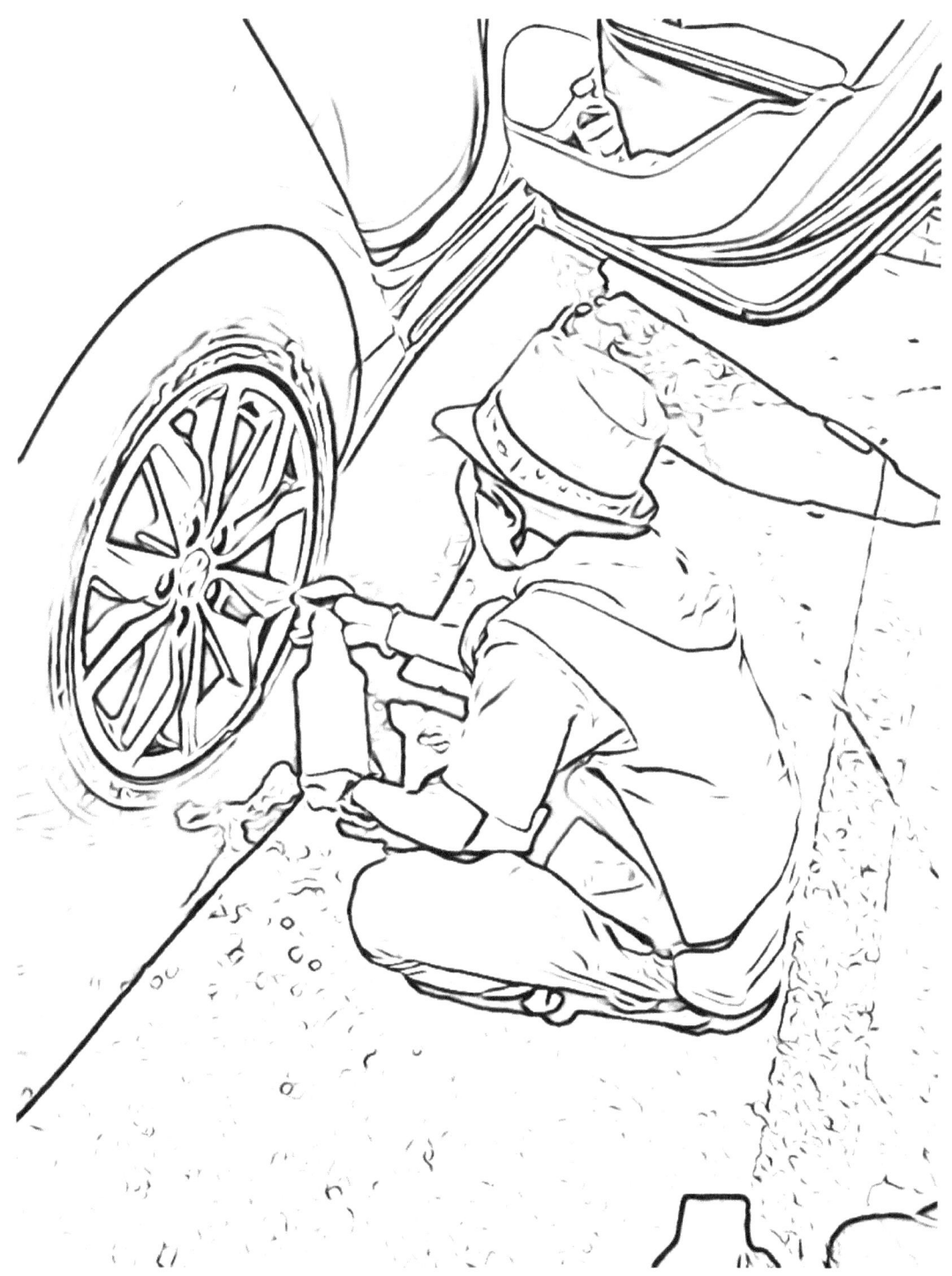

Nothing beats hard work. Weekends are spent teaching my son how to wash the car. Chivalry requires effort from both parties, not just receiving but contributing as well.

Chivalry Lives In You
Richard Patterson III

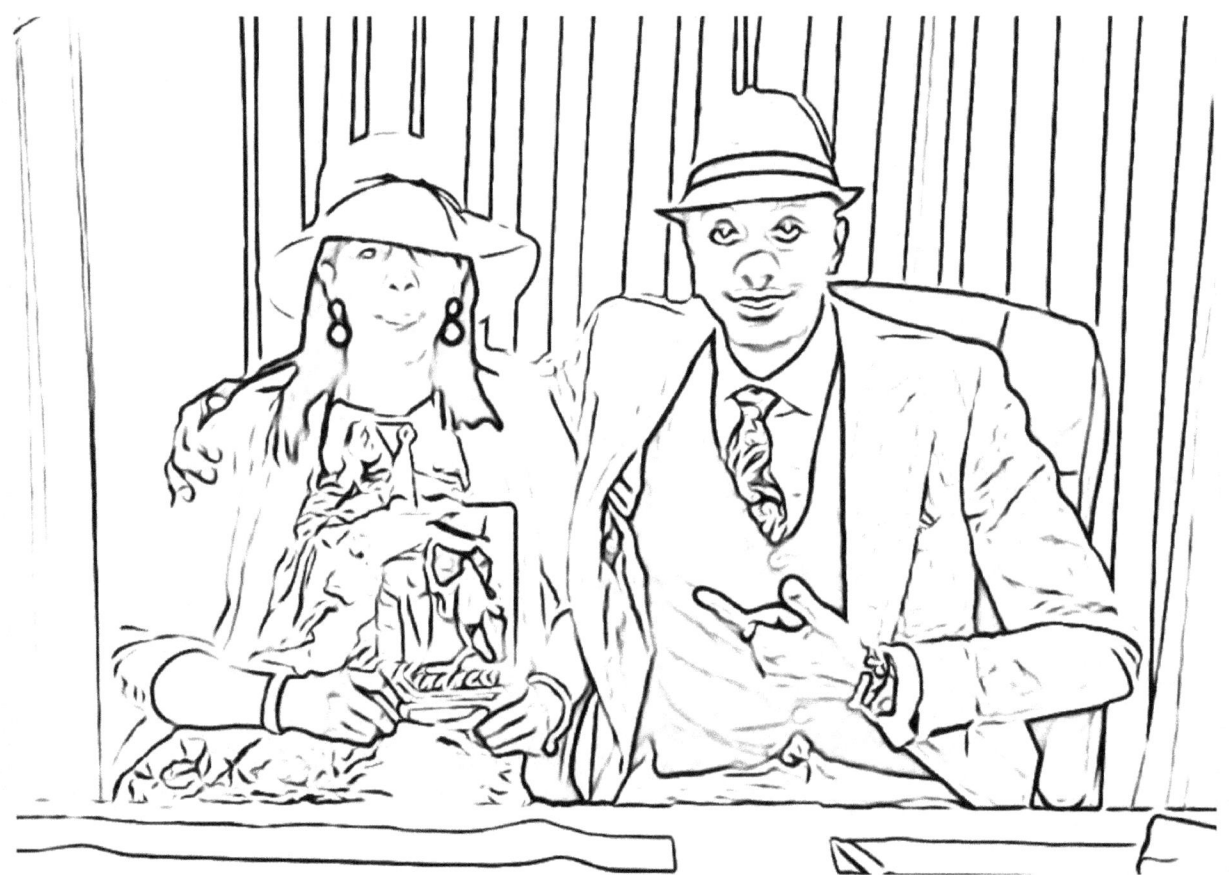

Children need to see what affection looks like in relationship. Chivalry shows up because it was taught and expressed through what the child observed. What he sees me do is what he will ultimately do in his relationships.

Chivalry Lives In You
Richard Patterson III

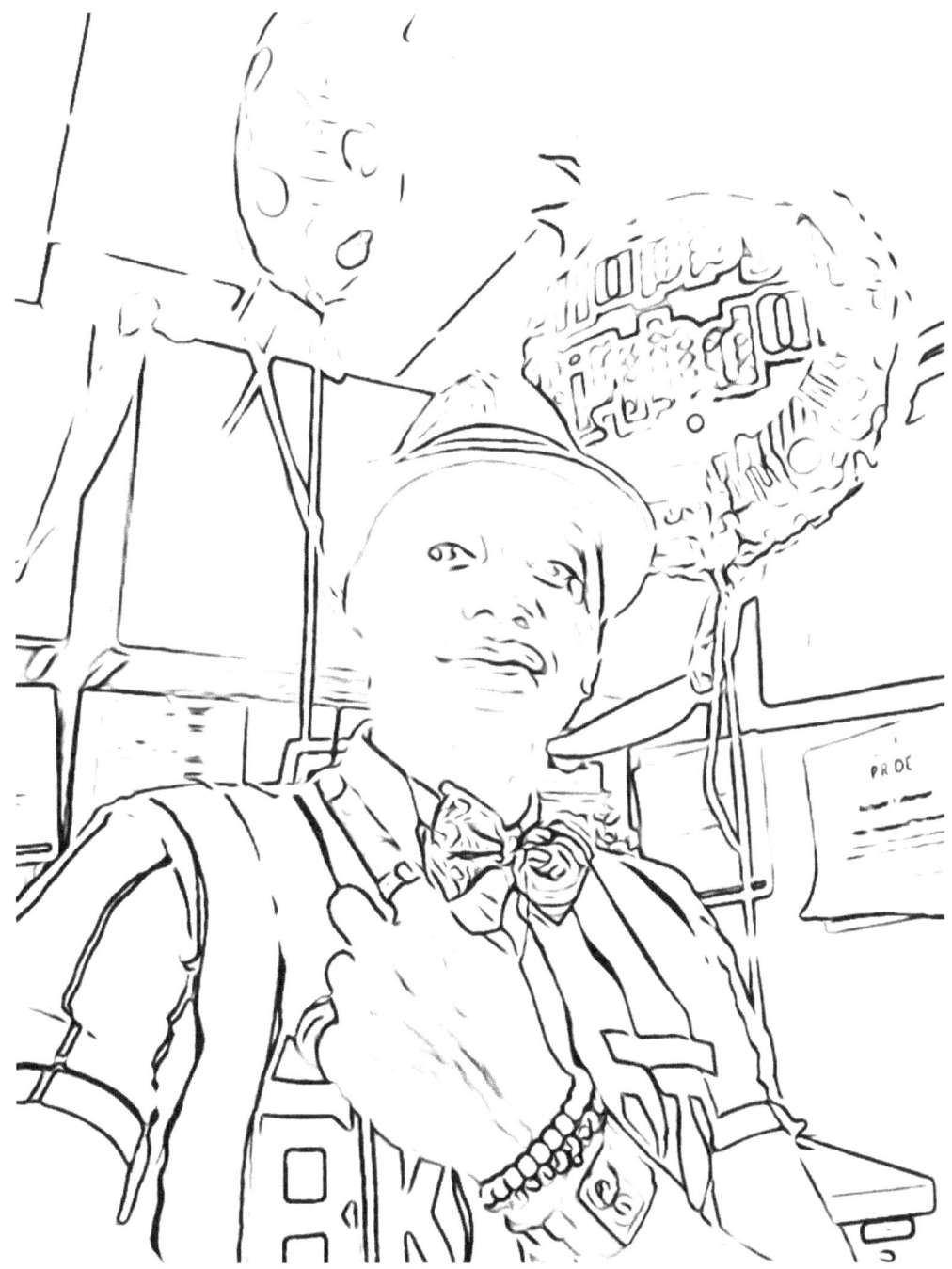

I like to celebrate special occasions with balloons. I'm teaching my son that special days in the lives of others are fun times. Chivalry is looking to celebrate others and sets the tone for being positive.

Chivalry Lives In You
Richard Patterson III

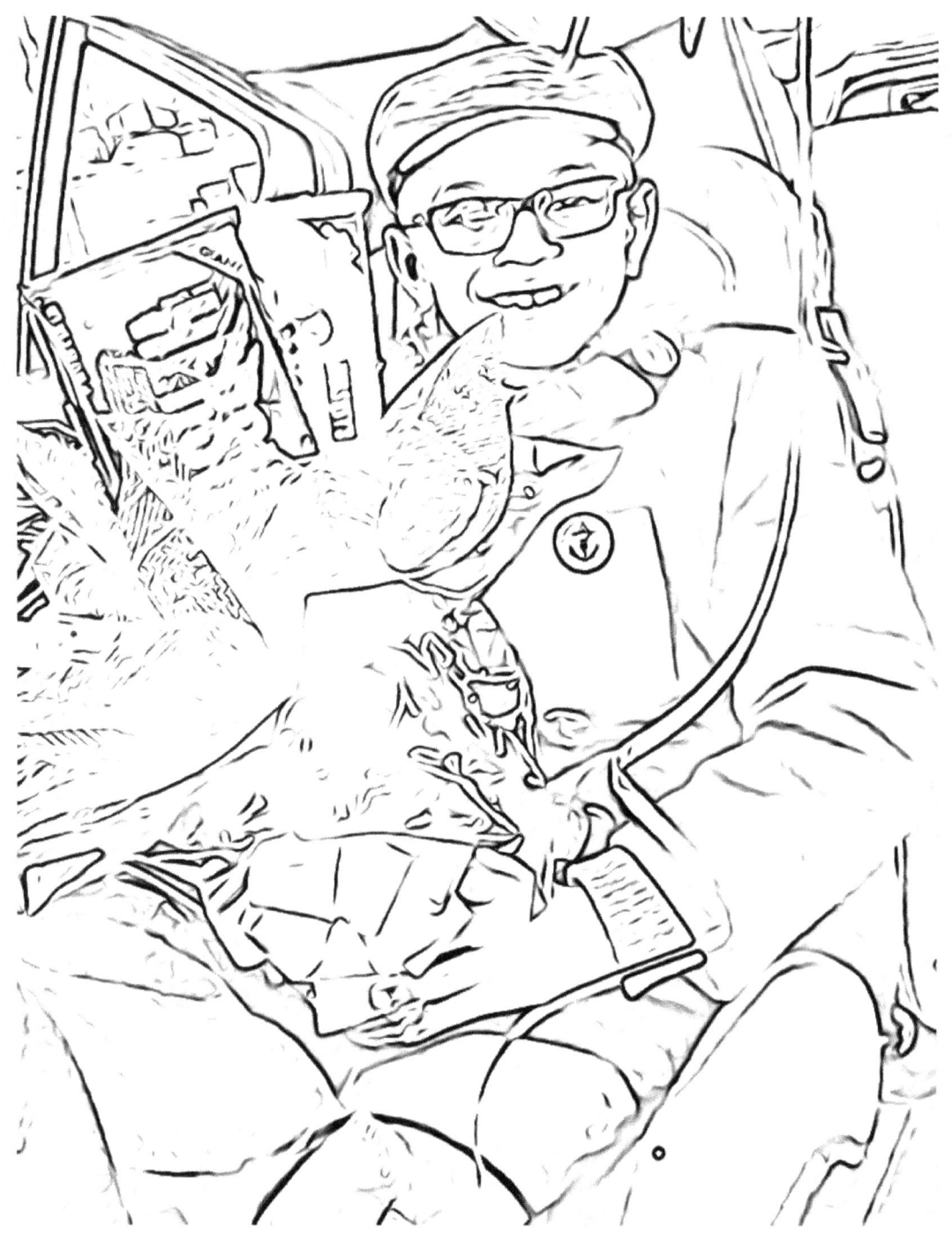

My son brings balloons and flowers to people he knows and to those he doesn't know. Chivalry seeks opportunity to acknowledge the value in others. Small and random acts of kindness

Chivalry Lives In You
Richard Patterson III

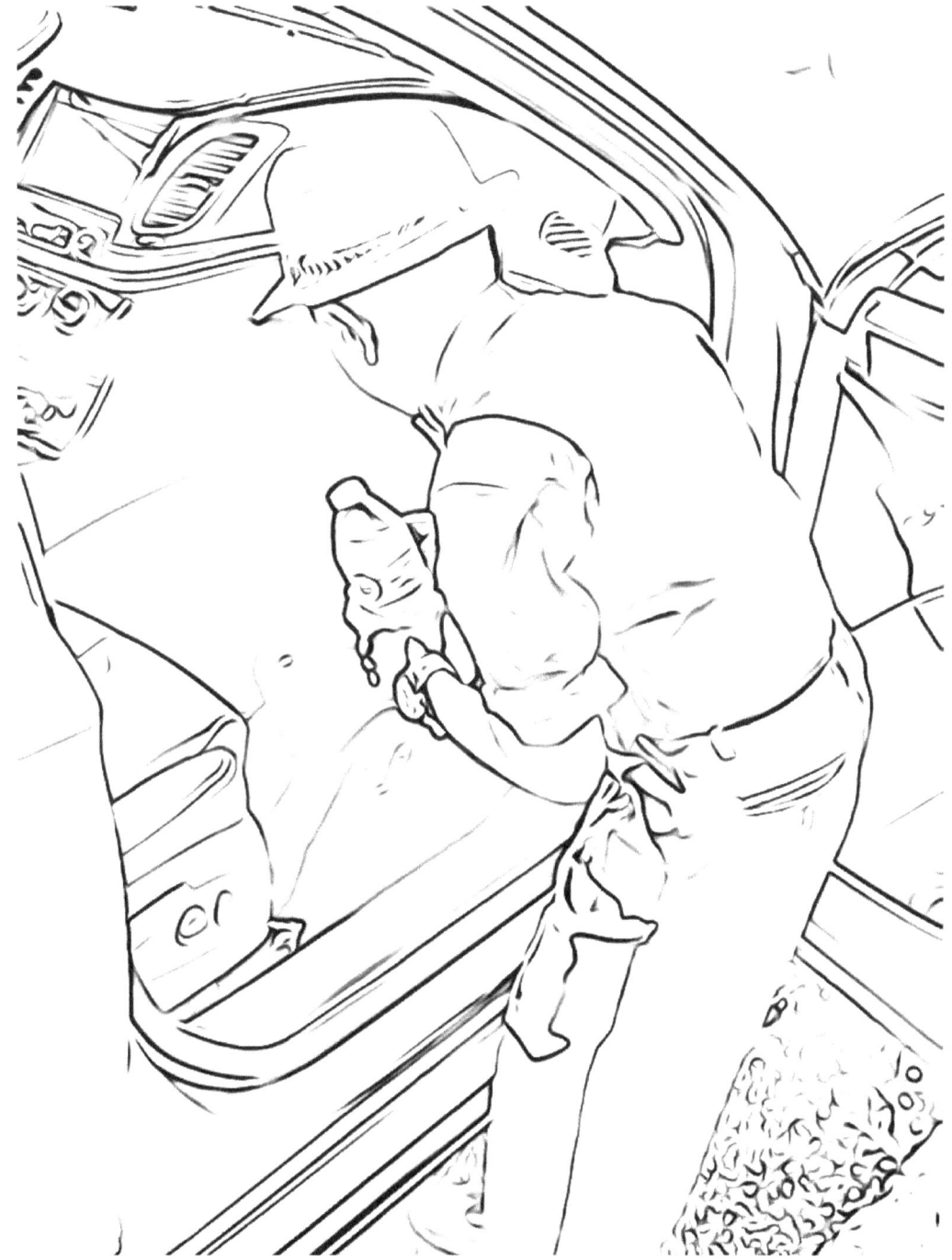

Taking the initiative to put the bags in the car is my son's way of helping his grandmother. Chivalry seeks to carry the load and is happy to serve.

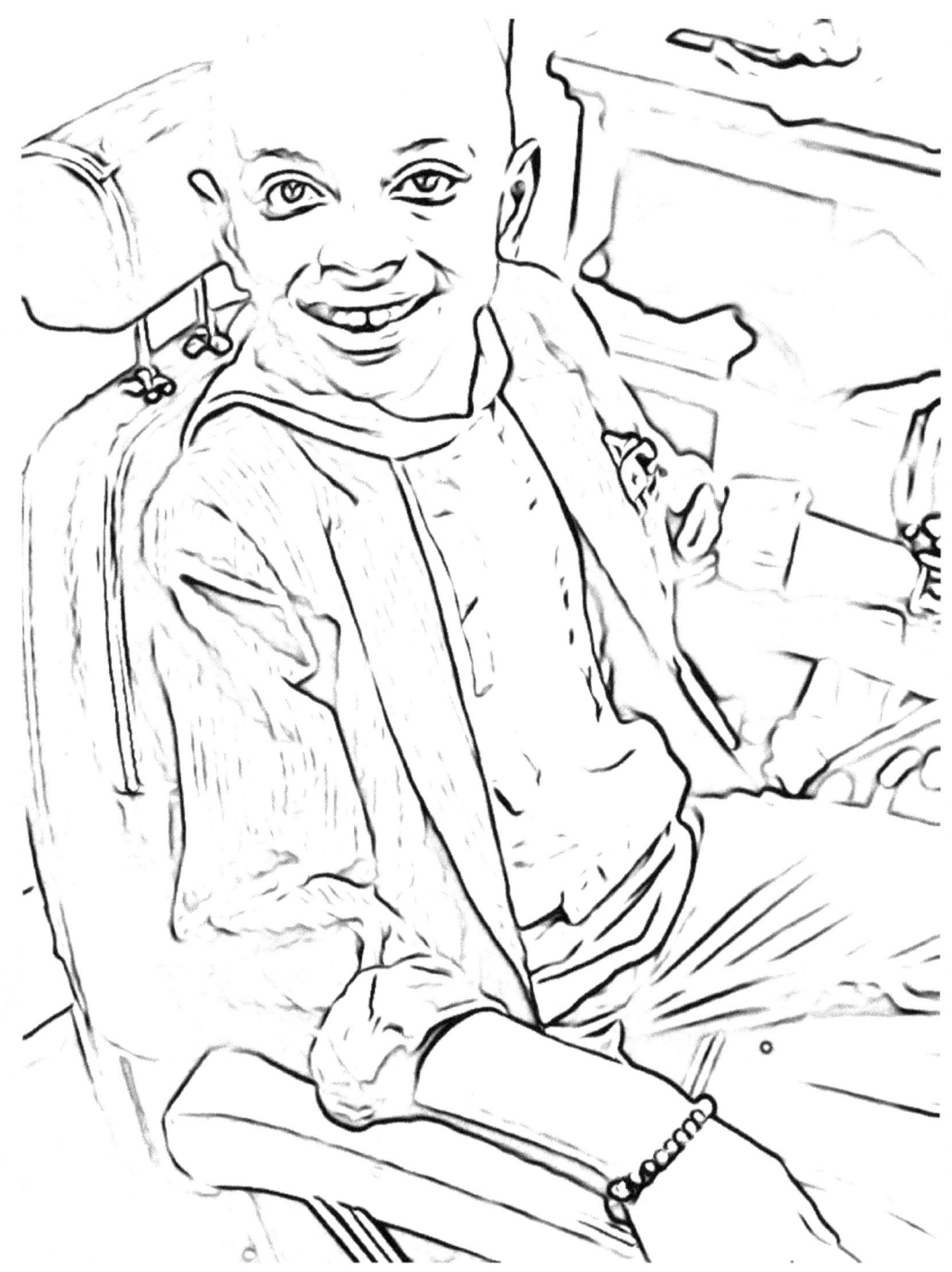

After my sons hair cut he sits and waits until my hair is cut. Chivalry is never in a hurry to run out but waits patiently to express gratitude.

Chivalry Lives In You
Richard Patterson III

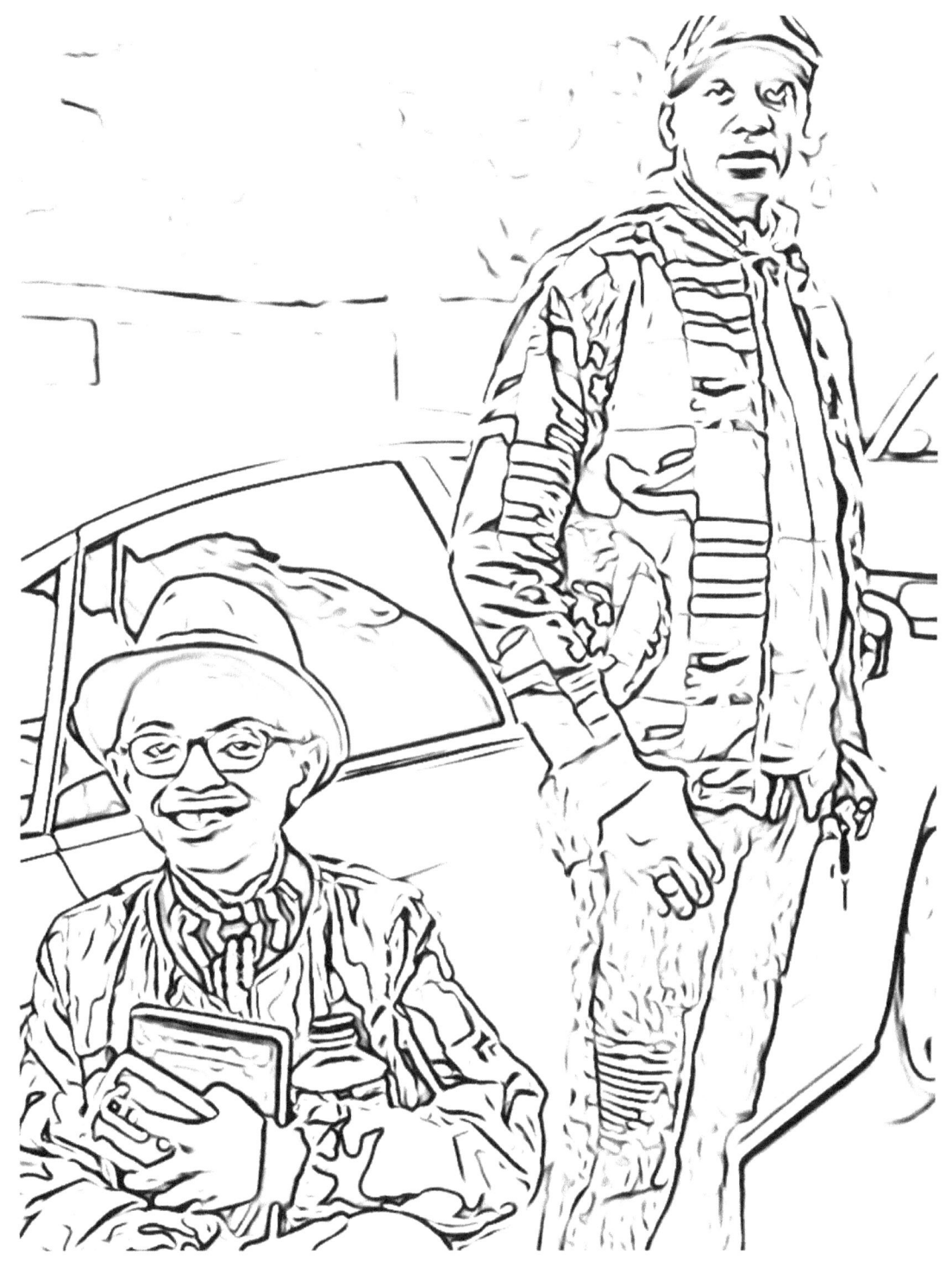

My son carries what he can carry understanding he can't do what I can do but he can contribute in his own way.

Coloring With Kindness, Page 21

Chivalry Lives In You
Richard Patterson III

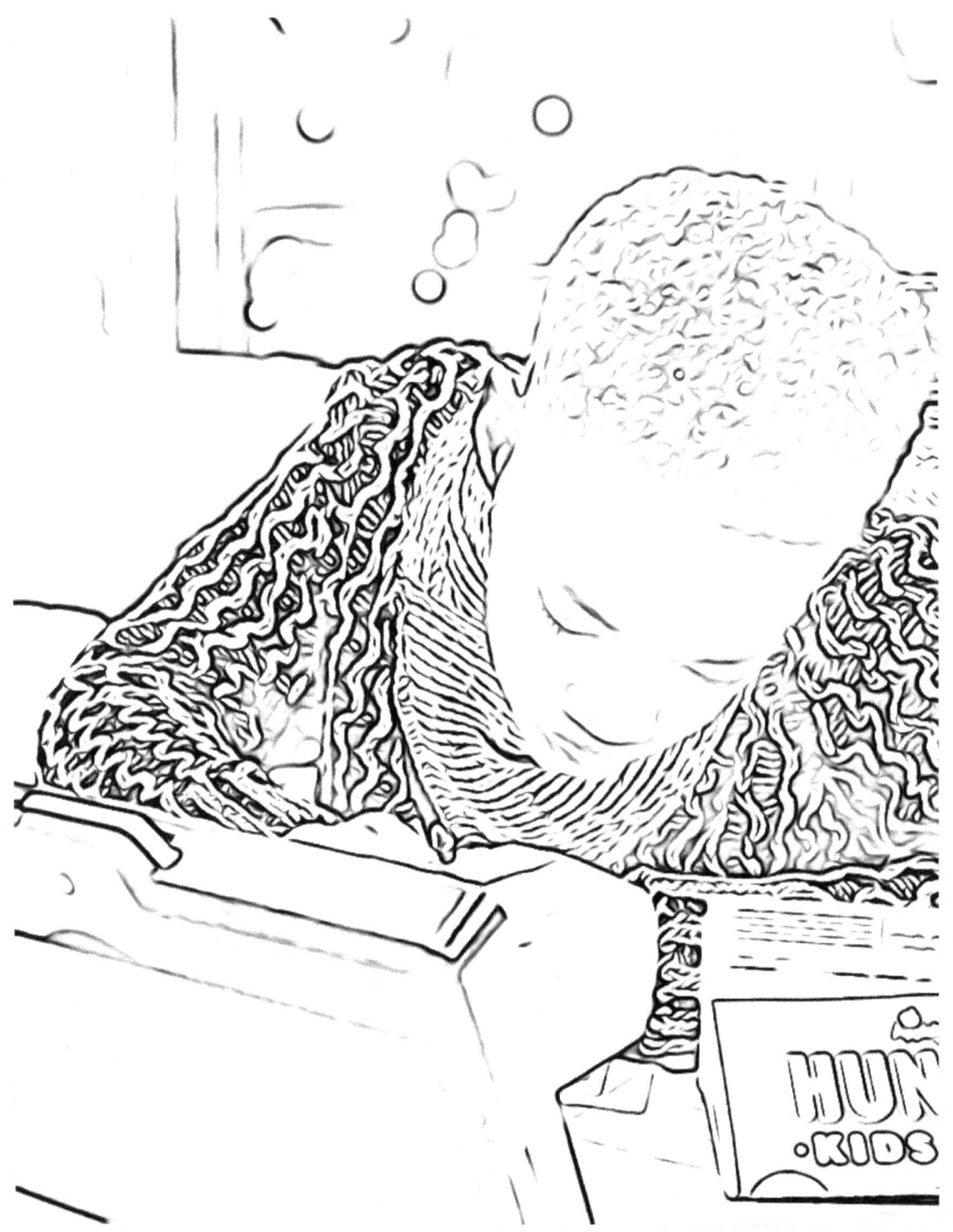

Every moment won't be about my son so he'll need to be able to share with others. Chivalry is an attitude that allows for other people to be the preference.

Chivalry Lives In You
Richard Patterson III

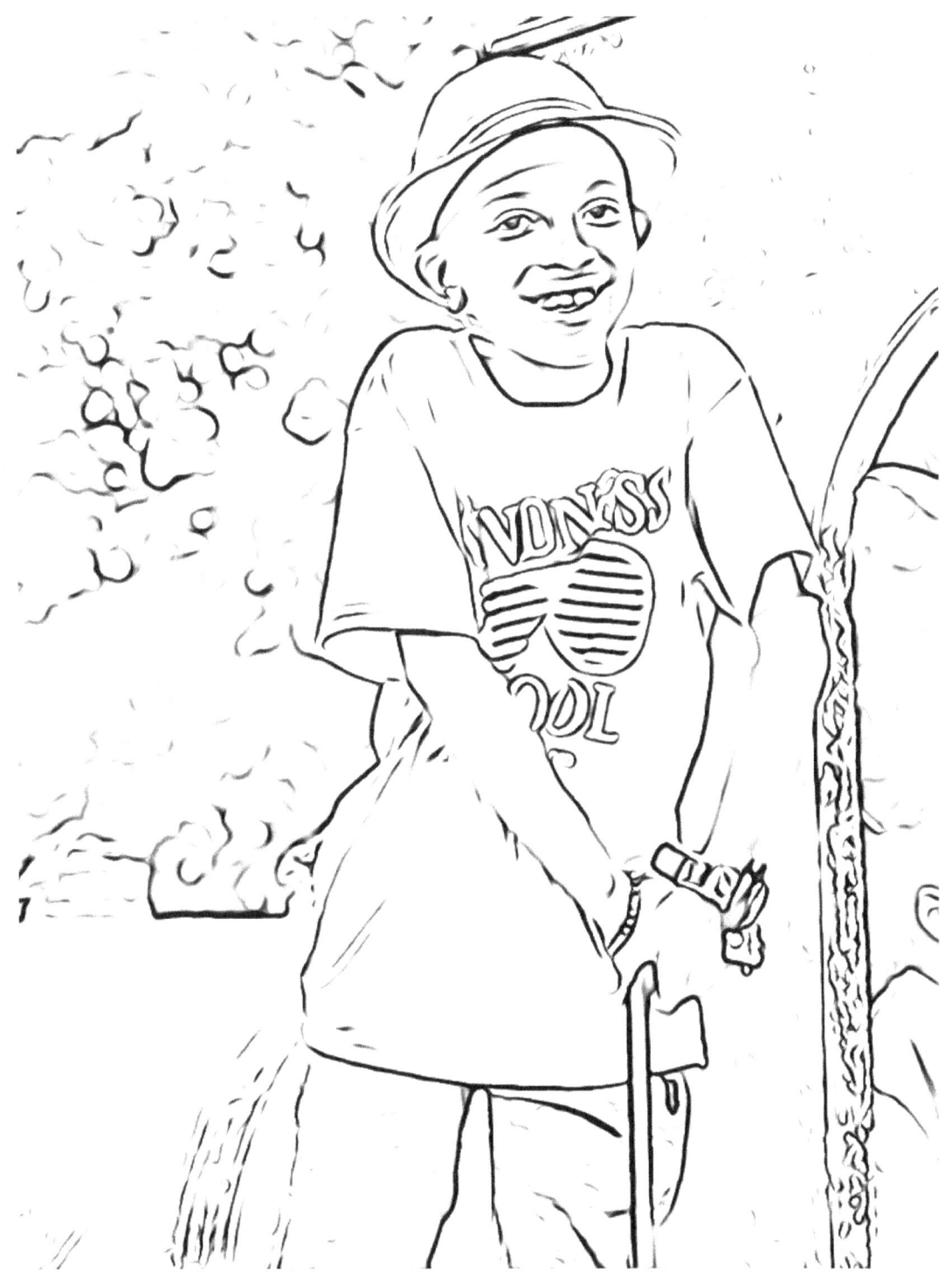

Good old fashion fun is necessary. Being light hearted allows you to express chivalry even in difficult times.

Chivalry Lives In You
Richard Patterson III

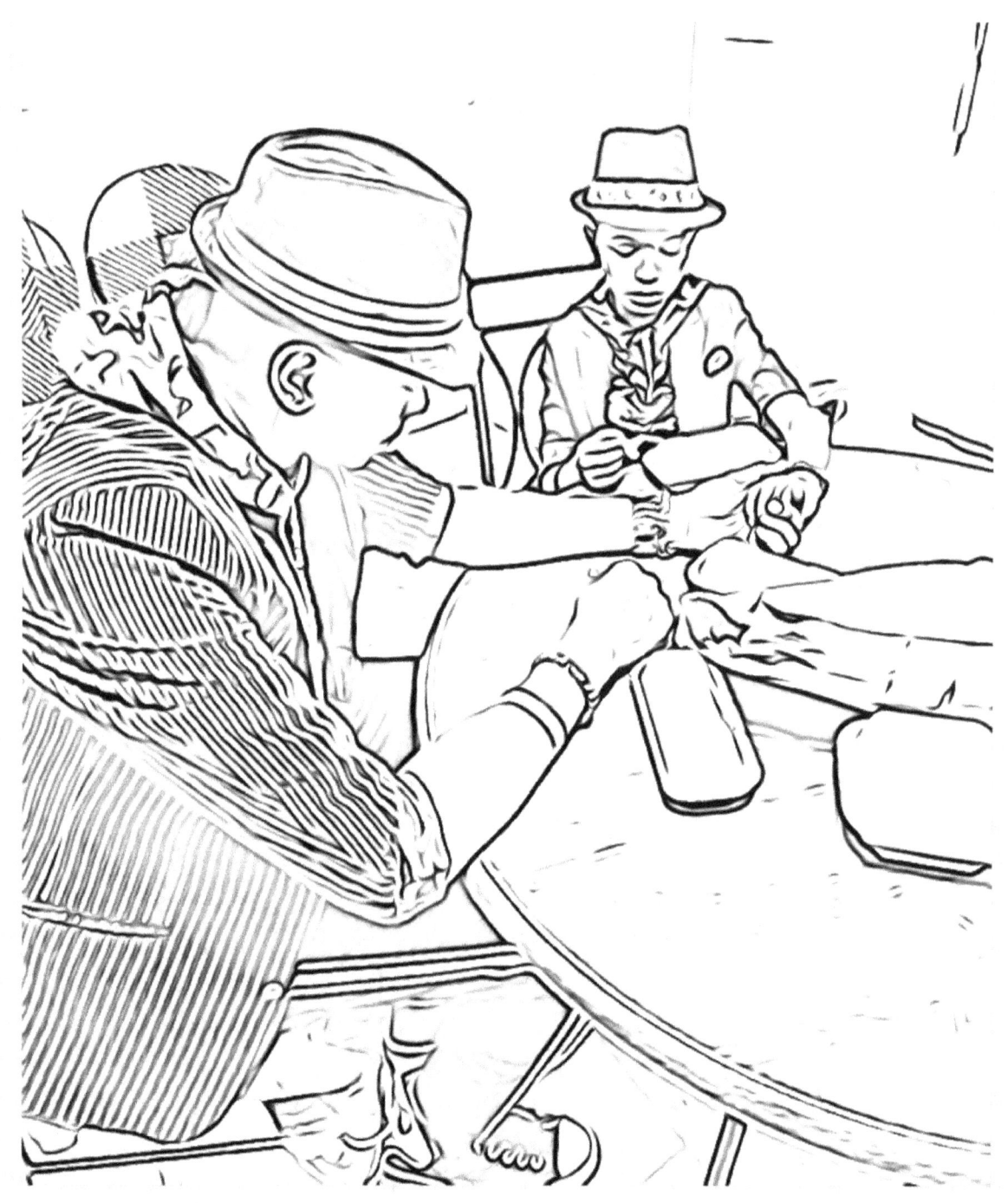

The dinner table is where conversations are had. He sees me and I see him. Chivalry means you understand someone could be having a bad day. So be Kind!!!

Chivalry Lives In You
Richard Patterson III

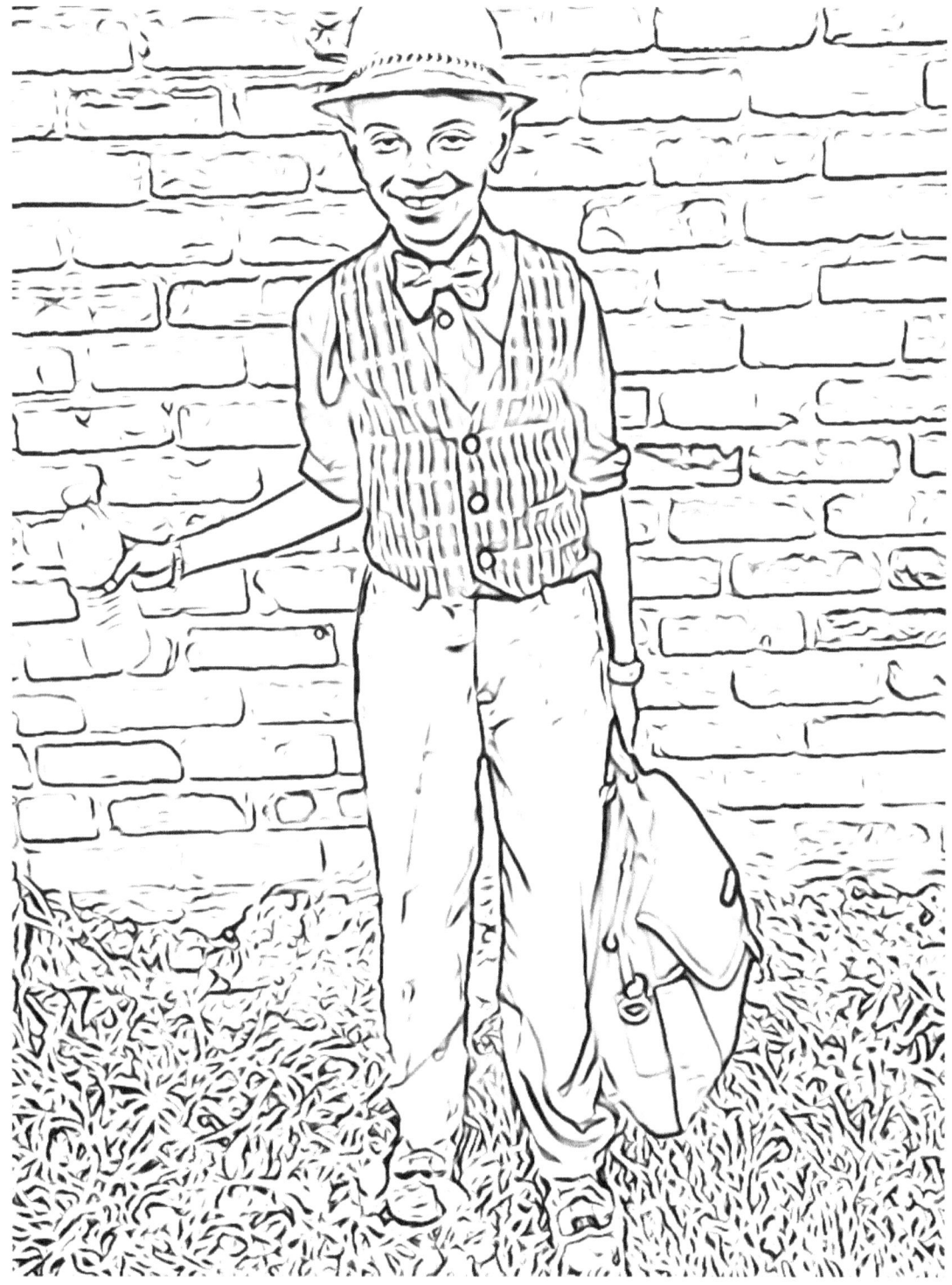

Chivalry becomes second nature, carrying the bag of others because you understand the weight of life.

Chivalry Lives In You
Richard Patterson III

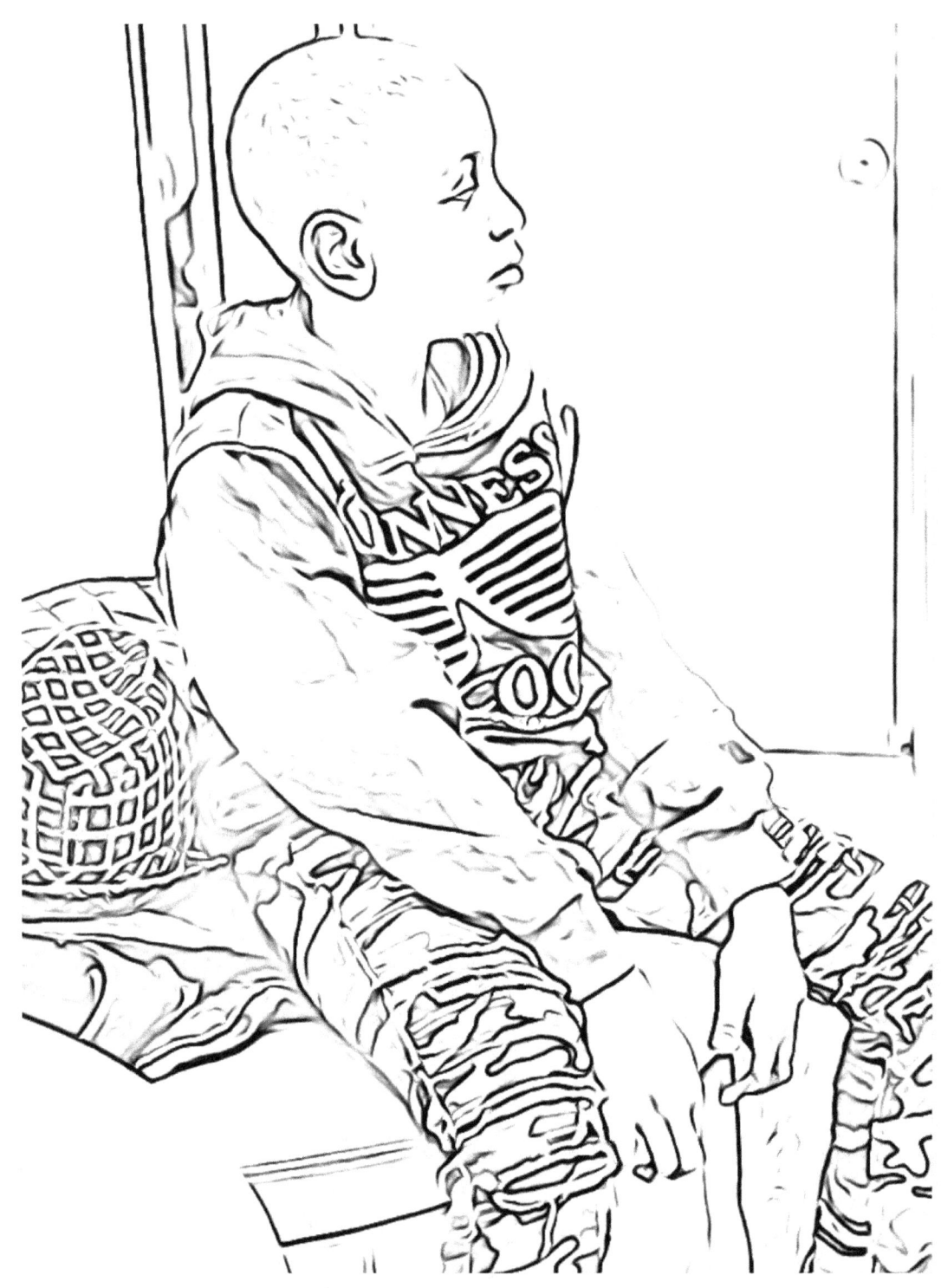

We watch documentaries at the barber shop and we talk faith, family and finances. Chivalry is all about hearing the need and supplying it.

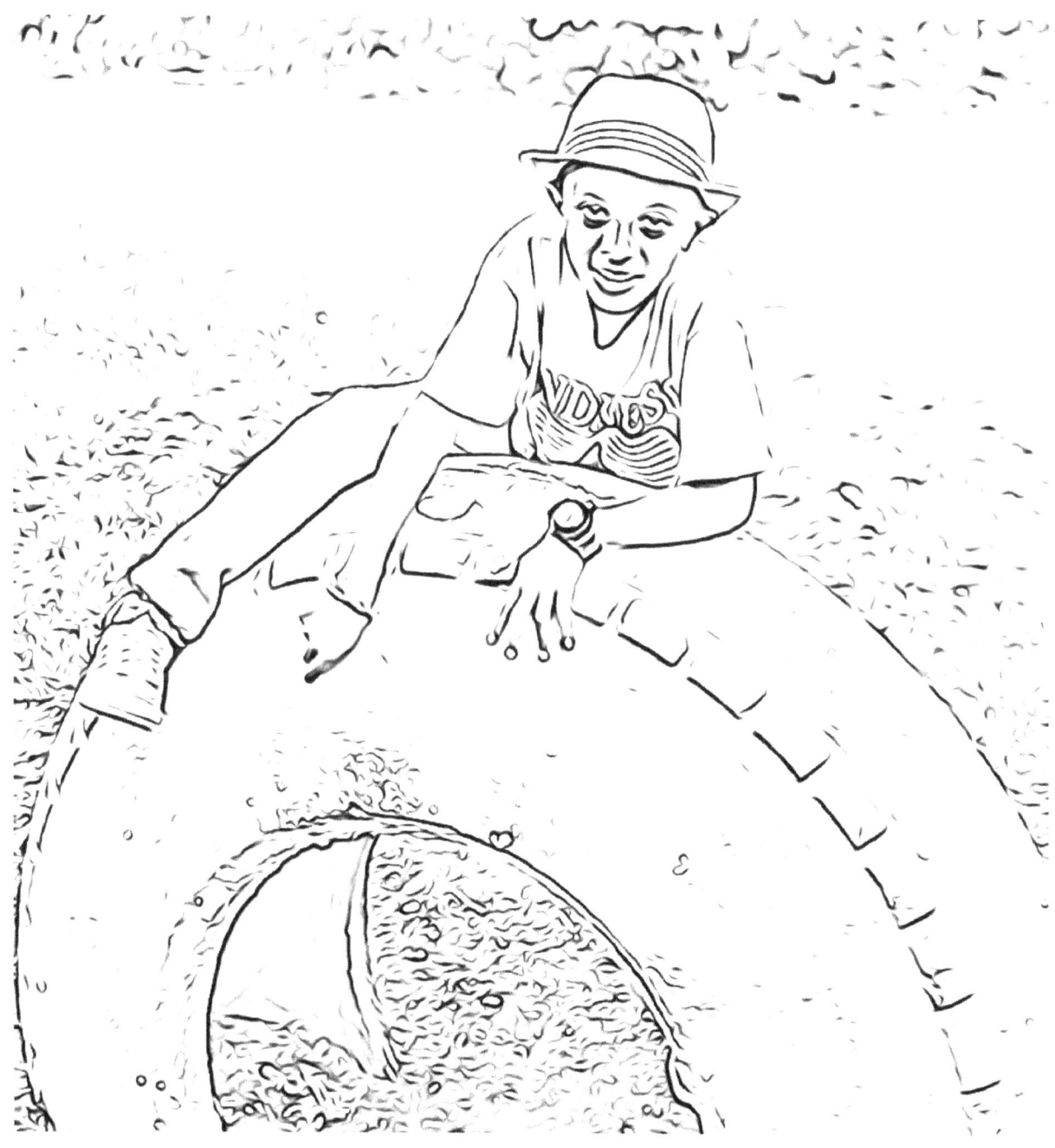

I have learned more about the character of my son while he was playing than any other time. Chivalry can be seen in times of recreation. How do you play with others?

Chivalry Lives In You
Richard Patterson III

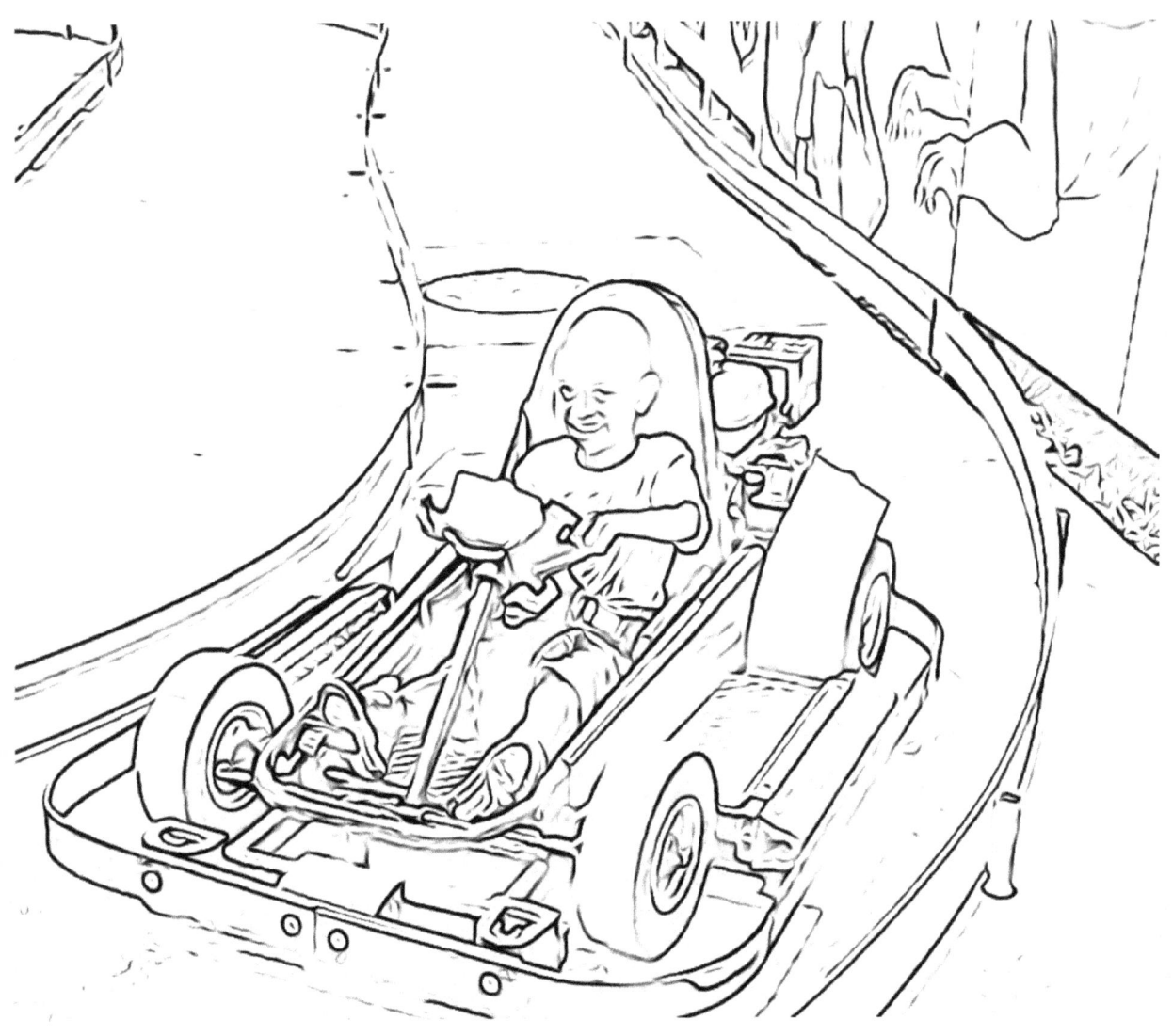

Like a race car on a track chivalry seeks to stay within the boundaries of respect even in times of recreation.

Chivalry Lives In You
Richard Patterson III

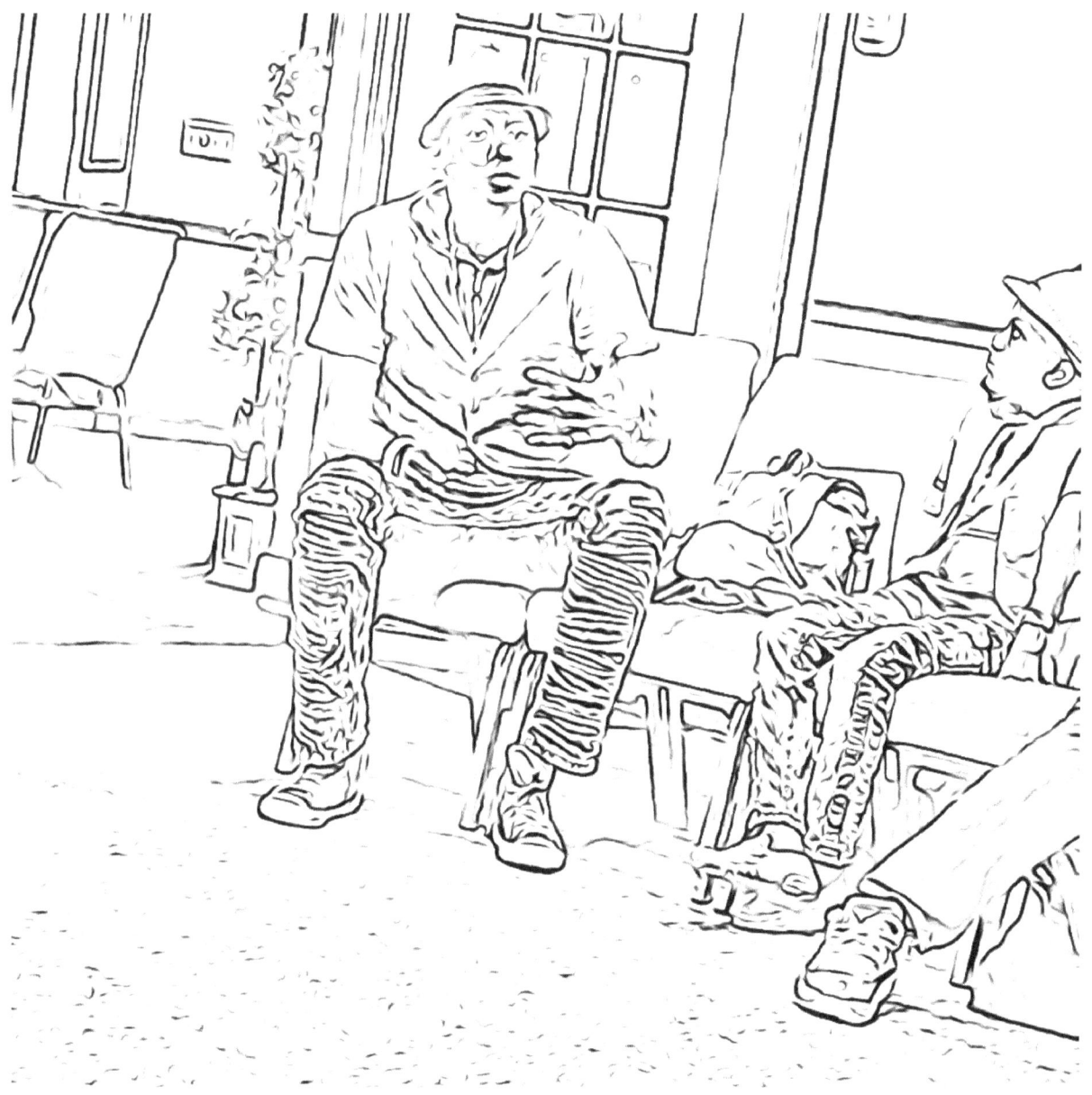

When you talk your children are listening to how you converse. Chivalry understands not everyone will agree with me, but I value your opinion enough to at least hear it.

Chivalry Lives In You
Richard Patterson III

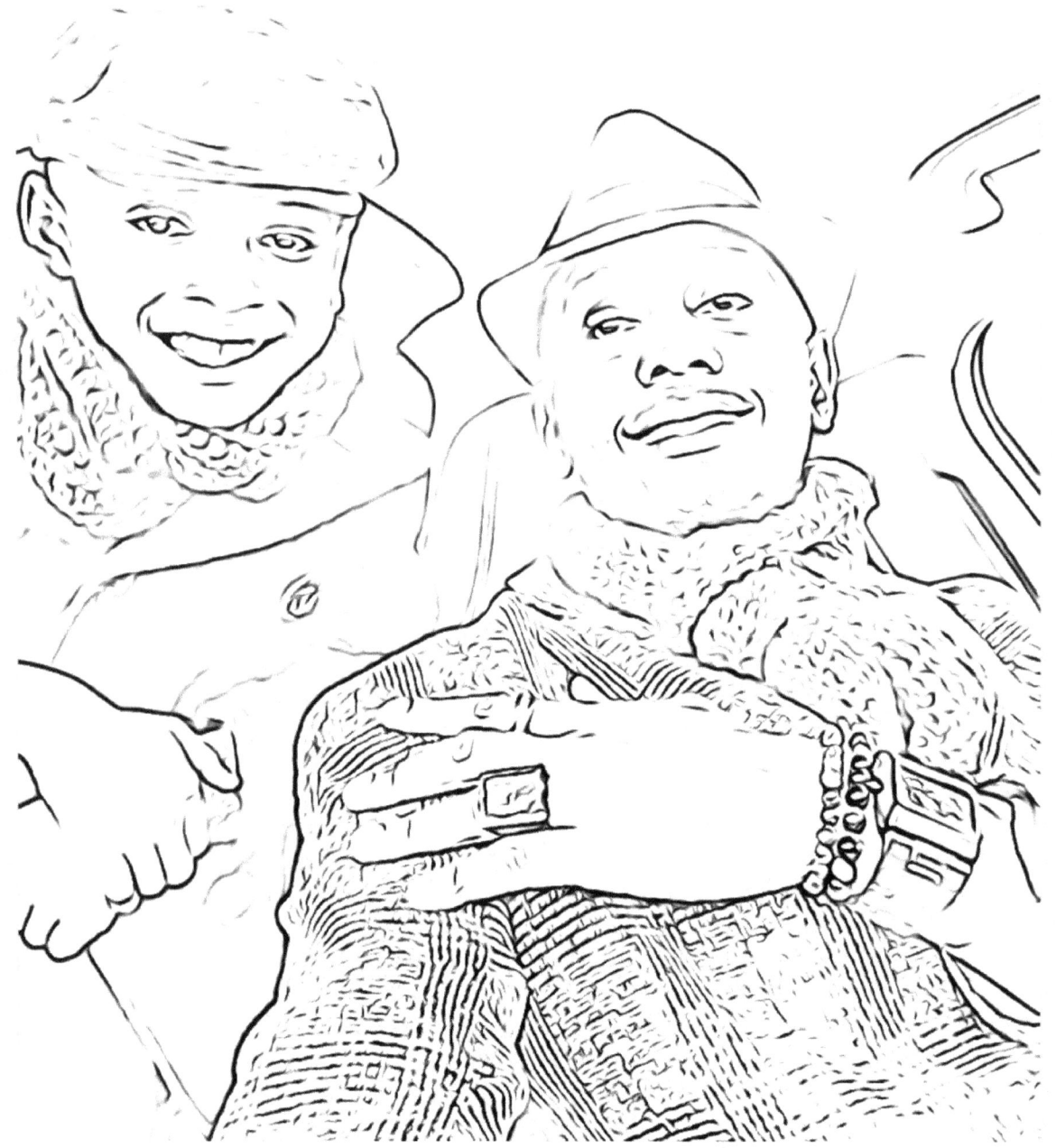

Laughing is essential, don't take things too personal. Chivalry is just happy to be alive and that joy is contagious and seeks to be shared with others.

Chivalry Lives In You
Richard Patterson III

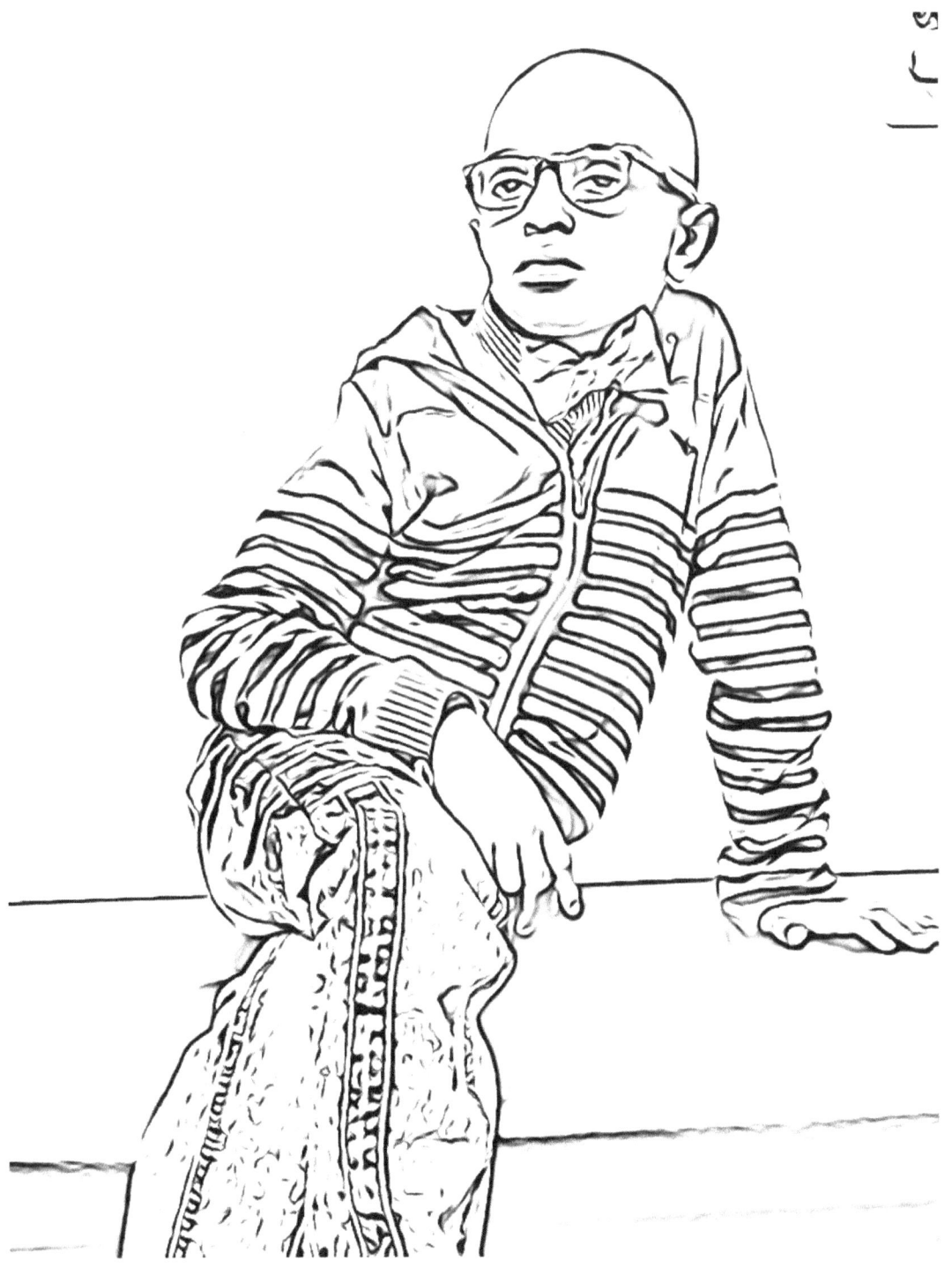

Chivalry like swag can be seen but unlike swag. Chivalry is not just a look but seeks to serve others with kindness.

Chivalry Lives In You
Richard Patterson III

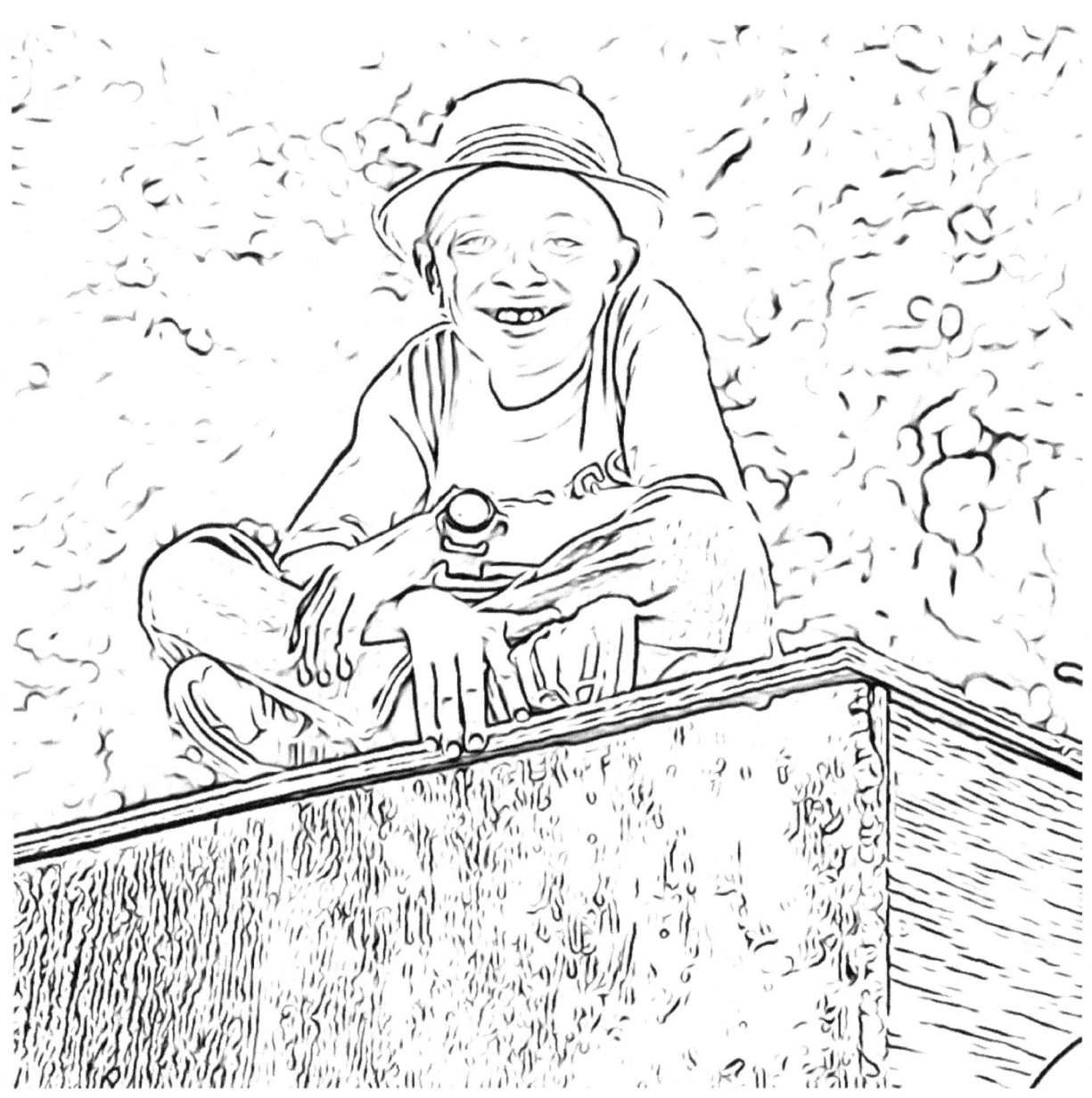

Chivalry is observant and takes the time to understand who's in the environment that needs help.

Coloring With Kindness , Page 32

Chivalry Lives In You
Richard Patterson III

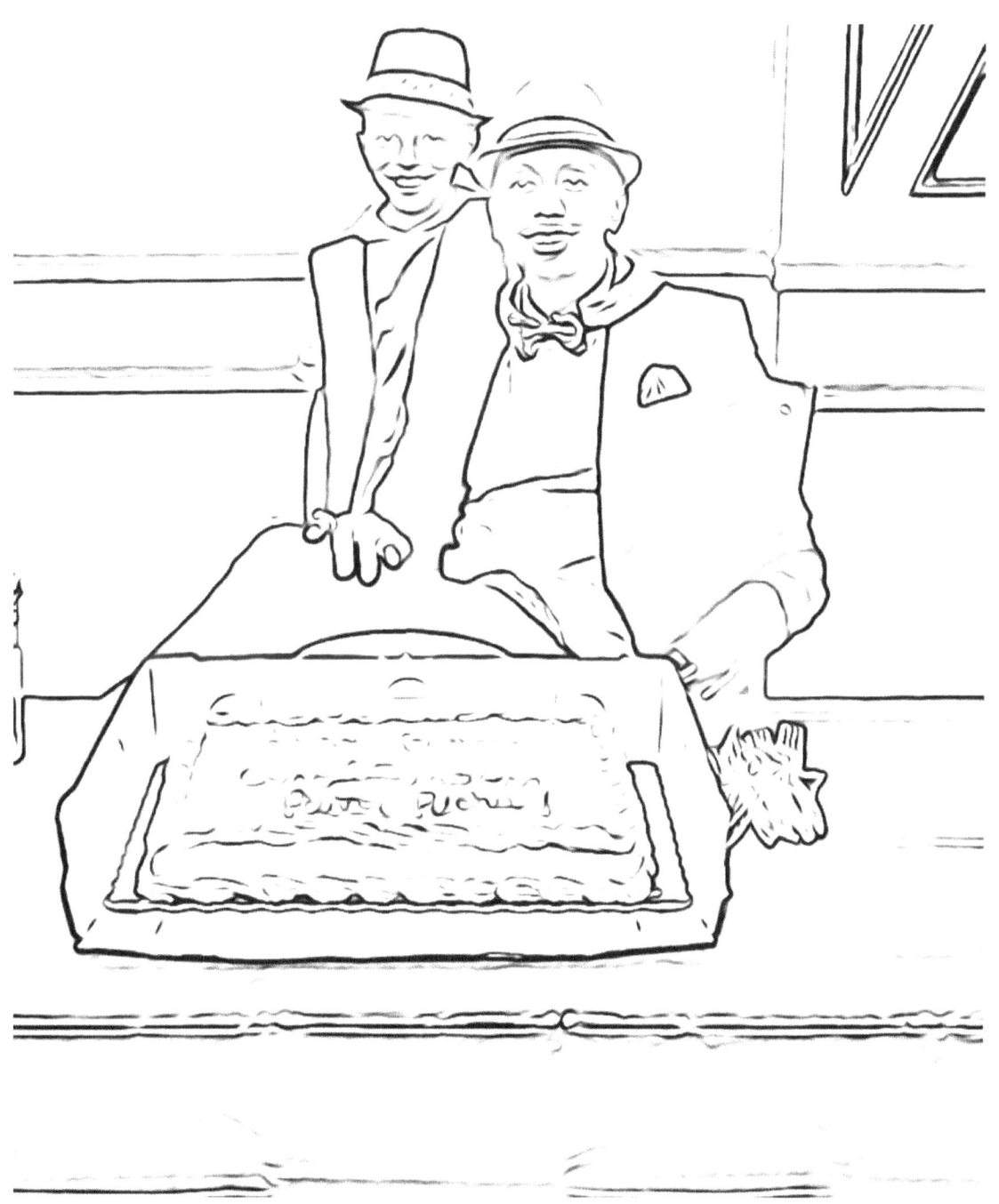

Like a birthday cake. Chivalry is not always wanted but like a piece of cake it's there for those who desire it. Never forced!!!!!

Chivalry Lives In You
Richard Patterson III

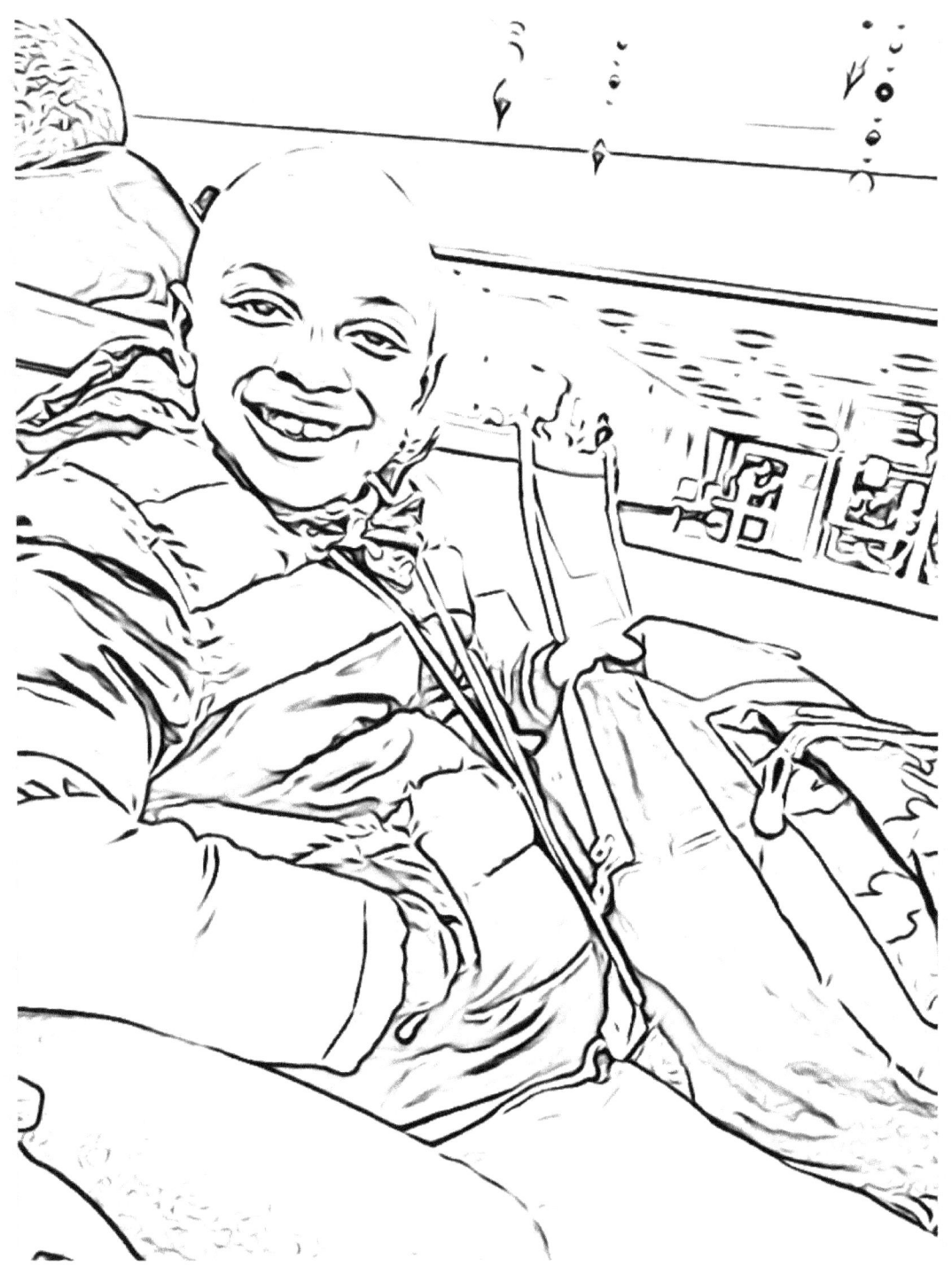

My son has his own personality wrapped in considering other people. Chivalry can be resurrected through training and quality time spent.

Chivalry Lives In You
Richard Patterson III

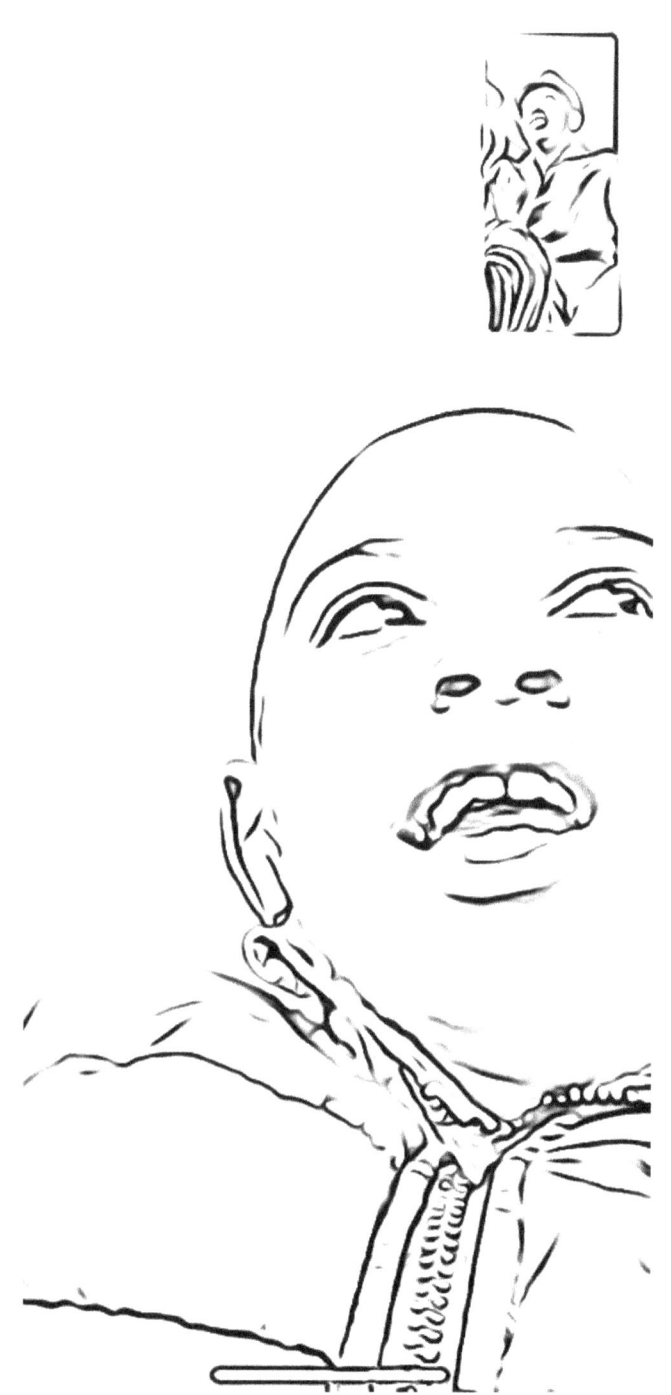

I don't like FaceTiming but because my son loves it. I engage him outside of my comfort zone. Chivalry shows up through making adjustments that best serve the relationship.

Chivalry Lives In You
Richard Patterson III

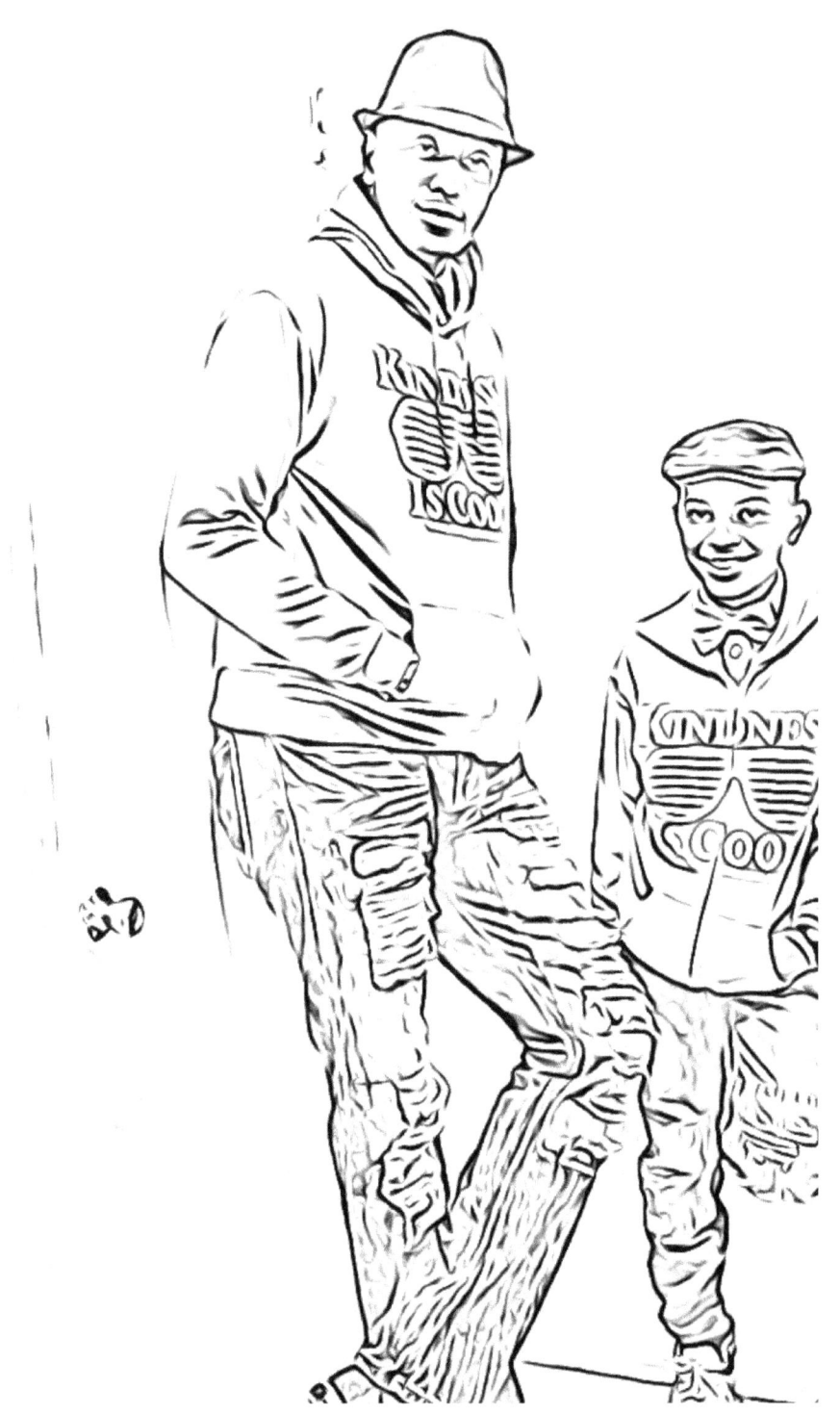

My greatest Joy as a father is knowing that my name lives on through how my son treats people with care.

Chivalry Lives In You
Richard Patterson III

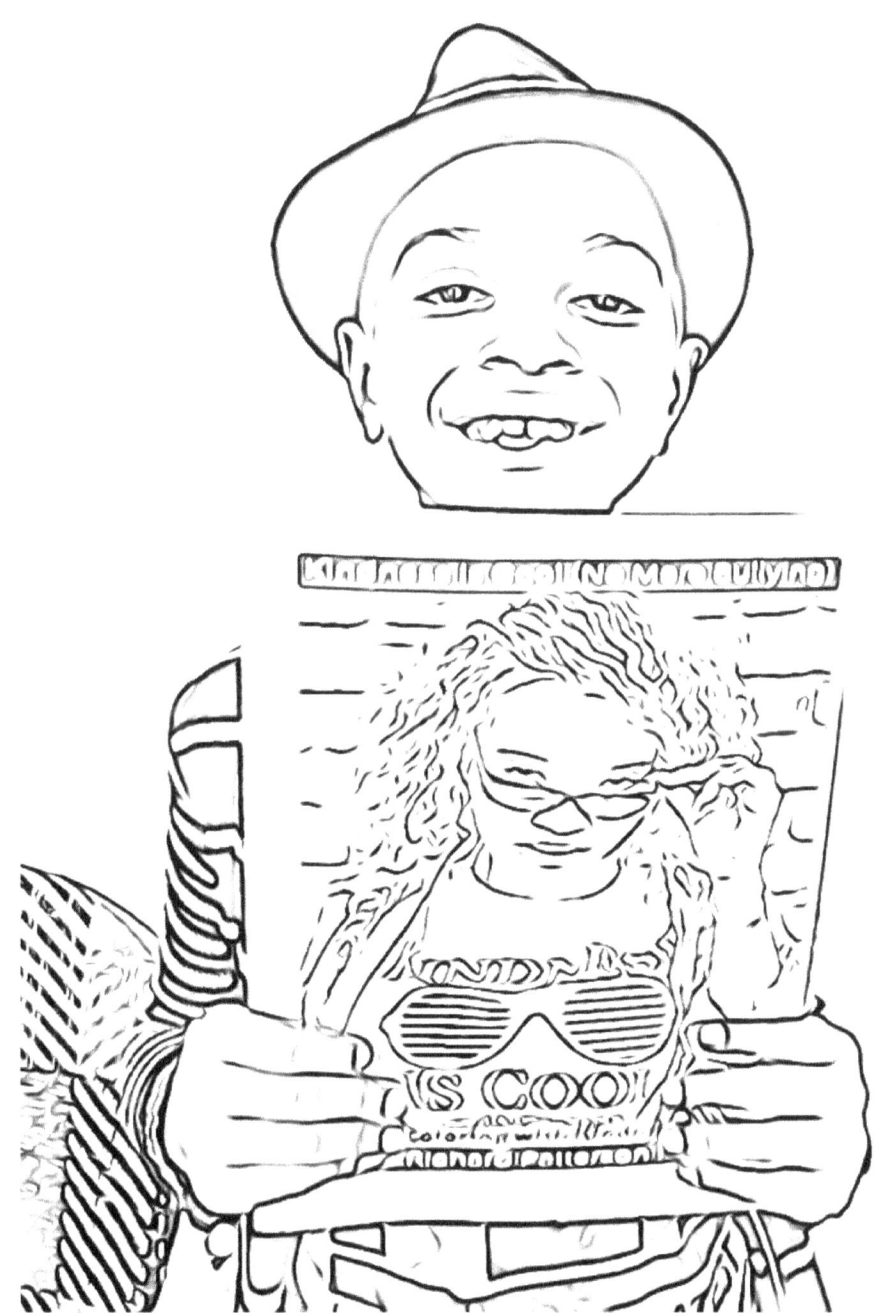

Kindness is an approach to establishing healthy relationships before challenges like Bullying occur. Chivalry keeps children grounded and focused on what can be done positively.

Coloring With Kindness, Page 37

Chivalry Lives In You
Richard Patterson III

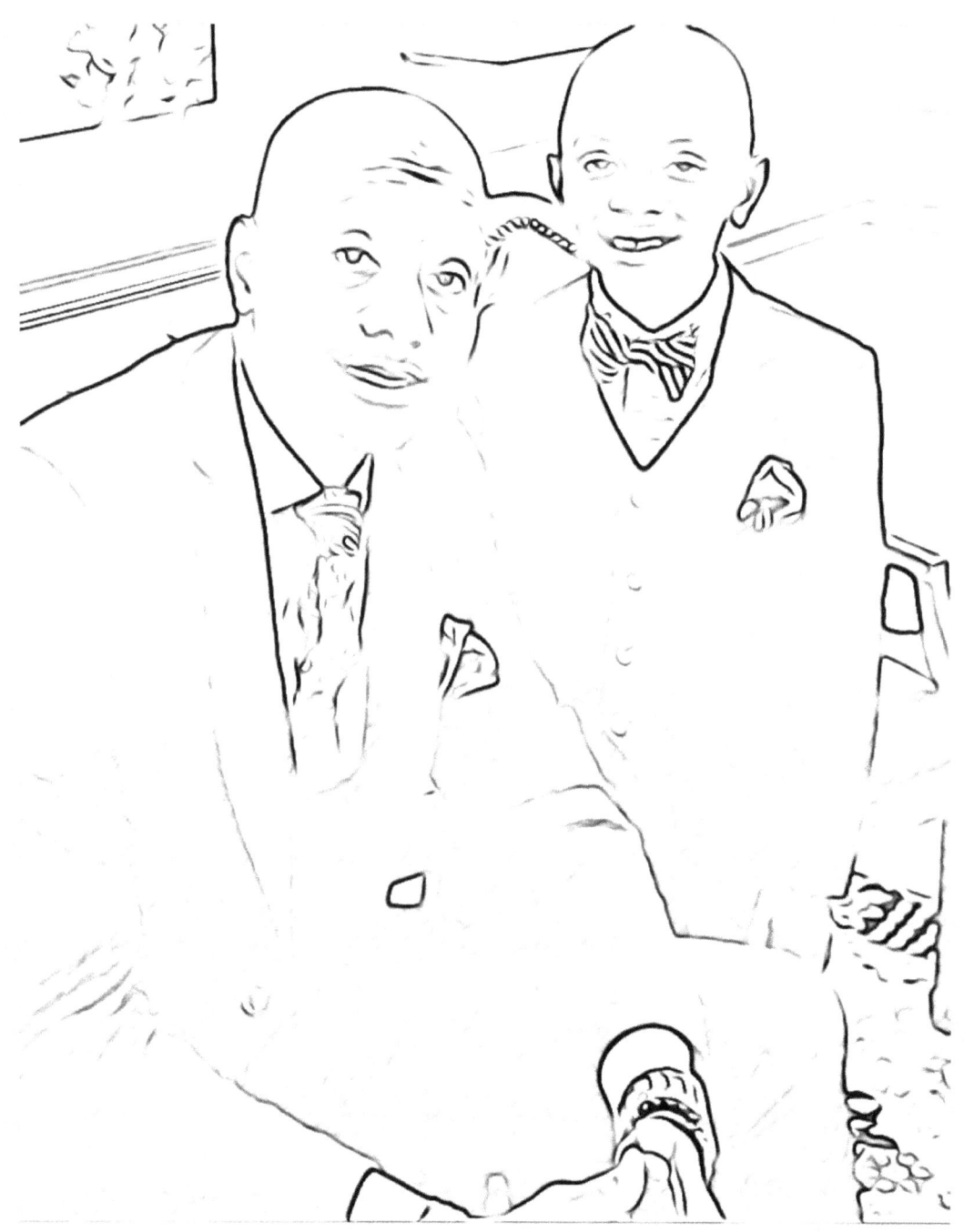

We work to leave an inheritance for our children, but more than a 401K. When we teach our children to care for human life that's legacy and it's value never depreciates.

Chivalry Lives In You
Richard Patterson III

Creating A Kind Culture

Kind Culture

www.richiepatterson.com

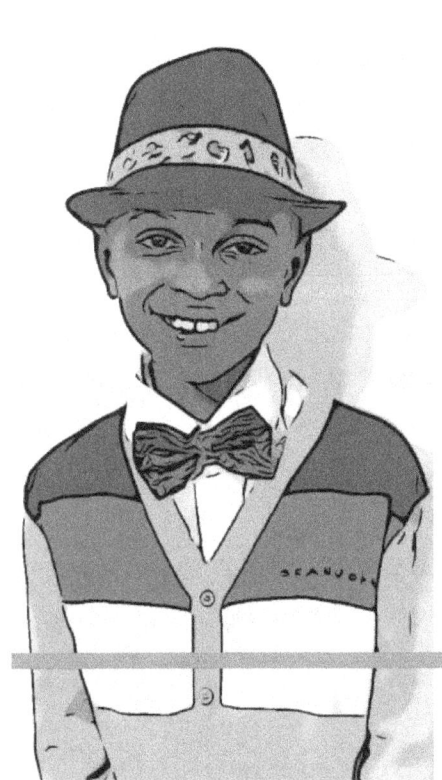

Developing focus and positive self esteem through Coloring

Cultivating Creativity through Coloring with Kindness
www.richiepatterson.com

#THISISTHEKINDNESS
#COLORINGWITHKINDNESS

Chivalry Lives In You
Richard Patterson III

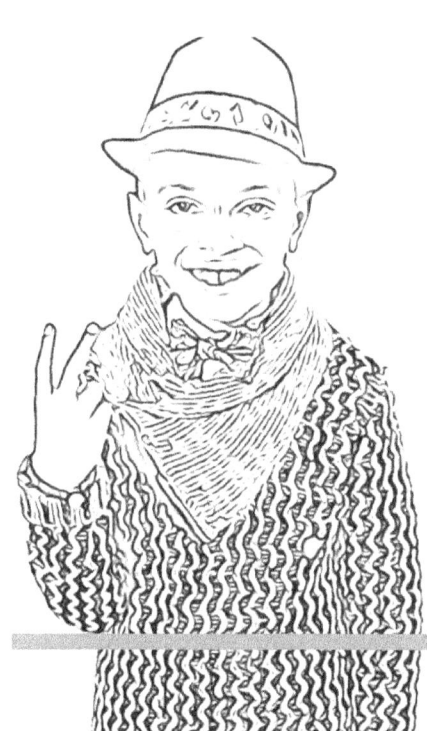

Gentlemen don't just show up but they were trained to value people. Chivalry lives in you

Cultivating Creativity through Coloring with Kindness
www.richiepatterson.com

#THISISTHEKINDNESS
#COLORINGWITHKINDNESS

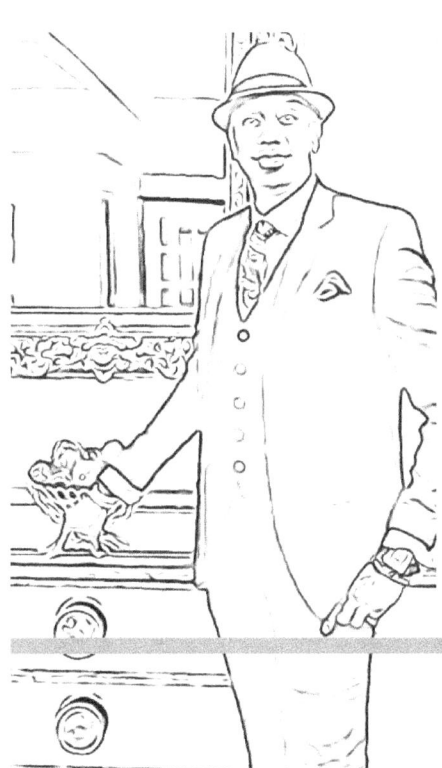

Available for Workshops, Speaking Engagements, Open Forums, Counseling Sessions And More

Pastor Richie Patterson III
8225 Allen Rd #1018
Allen Park, MI 48101
248.372.9500
www.richiepatterson.com

#THISISTHEKINDNESS
#COLORINGWITHKINDNESS

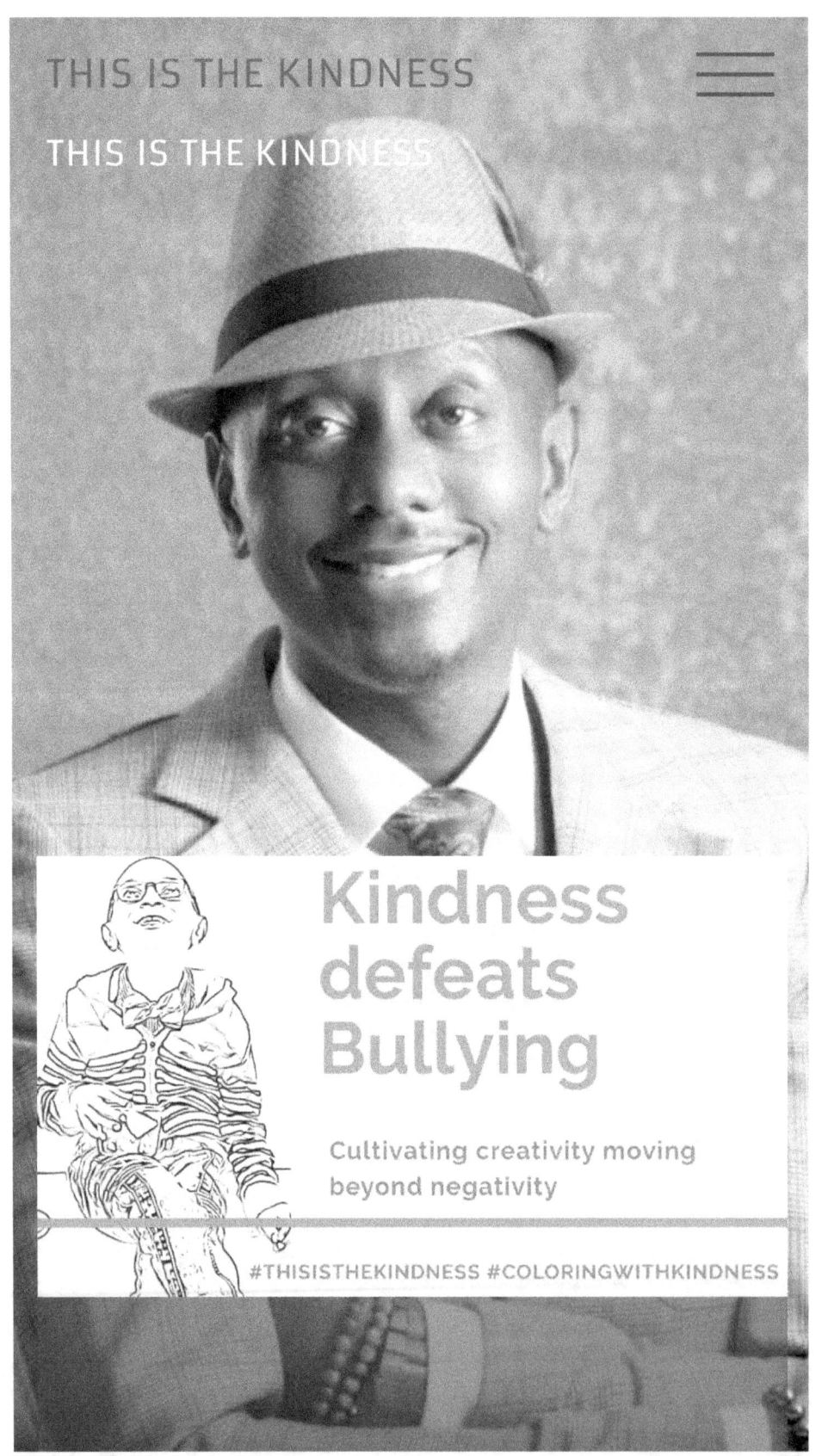

Chivalry Lives In You
Richard Patterson III

Chivalry Lives In You
Richard Patterson III

Coloring With Kindness, Page 46

www.ingramcontent.com/pod-product-compliance
Lightning Source LLC
Chambersburg PA
CBHW062343220526
45469CB00008B/2822